DATE

THE LIBRARY OF WORLD AFFAIRS

Editors:
GEORGE W. KEETON
AND
GEORG SCHWARZENBERGER

Number 38

DEMOCRATIC INSTITUTIONS
IN THE WORLD TODAY

AUSTRALIA
The Law Book Co. of Australasia Pty Ltd.
Sydney : Melbourne : Brisbane

GREAT BRITAIN
Stevens & Sons Limited
London

INDIA
N. M. Tripathi Private Ltd.
Bombay

NEW ZEALAND
Sweet and Maxwell (N.Z.) Ltd.
Wellington

PAKISTAN
Pakistan Law House
Karachi

U.S.A. AND CANADA
Frederick A. Praeger, Inc.
New York City

Democratic Institutions
in
The World Today

Editor
WERNER BURMEISTER

Published under the auspices of
THE LONDON INSTITUTE OF WORLD AFFAIRS

NEW YORK
FREDERICK A. PRAEGER, INC.
1958

BOOKS THAT MATTER

*Published in the United
States of America in 1958
by Frederick A. Praeger,
Inc., Publishers, of 15
West 47th Street, New
York 36, N.Y.*

*Library of Congress
Catalog Card. No. 58–8175*

*First published in 1958 by
Stevens & Sons Limited
of 119 & 120 Chancery Lane
London — Law Publishers
and printed in Great Britain
by Bradford & Dickens of
Drayton House, London, W.C.1*

CONTENTS

CONTRIBUTORS

Werner Burmeister

Staff Tutor in International Relations,
Department of Extra-Mural Studies,
University of London

Bernard Lewis

Professor of the History of the Near and Middle East,
School of Oriental and African Studies,
University of London

Roland Oliver

Lecturer in African History,
School of Oriental and African Studies,
University of London

Richard H. Pear

Lecturer in Political Science,
London School of Economics and Political Science,
University of London

Hugh Tinker

Lecturer in the History of South East Asia,
School of Oriental and African Studies,
University of London

PREFACE

THE lectures published here were delivered at a course which the Department of Extra-Mural Studies in the University of London organised, early in 1957, in co-operation with the National Peace Council. The suggestion to collect and publish these papers came from the London Institute of World Affairs. To all of these I should like to express my gratitude for the help they have so readily given.

The character and scope of this publication are determined by its origin. It does not by any means survey democratic institutions in all the countries where they exist. Only the chapter on the United States has been added to the lectures included in the original course. And since British democratic institutions do not get any special treatment, it may be seen that the book is at least impartial in its omissions. The reasons for the inclusion of China, when so much of the non-Communist world has had to be left out, emerge from the second of the two chapters on Asia. It will also explain why so large a share of the space has gone to a continent whose future political development will have vital repercussions in all the rest of the world.

Each contributor has of course applied his own interpretation and drawn his own conclusions and is therefore responsible only for these. The broad agreement which nevertheless emerges evidently springs from the subject matter and the nature of the situation in which we find ourselves.

We are often only too ready to perceive the dangers and anxieties arising from the precarious balance of forces in the world today, and to complain about the burdens involved in maintaining that balance. We are less ready to remember that, on several occasions after 1945, it seemed doubtful whether we should even be granted such a period of troubled co-existence. The co-operation of the West has made it possible to check the military threat. This, although it remains absolutely indispensable, can only be a first step. If we have now entered upon a period of prolonged military stalemate, the great contest between democratic progress and Communism is brought back to the field of politics. It is likely to be decided in terms of political ideas and constructive achievements.

Any consideration of democracy in the modern world raises the question of what adjustments may be necessary, not merely in our political machinery but in our political approach, now that the West is losing its position of superiority. Large parts of the world are rapidly changing their character under the impact both of nationalism and industrialisation. They are, most of them, doing so by methods very different from those that helped to shape the social structure and political habits of western countries. There is no adequate accumulation of capital as the result of individual enterprise, no gradual emergence of an independent middle class which can claim and obtain the right not only to shape its own destiny but that of the whole of society. There is no working class accustomed to look upon the defence and development of free institutions as the only way of securing its own economic and social advance.

That is why it would be short-sighted and useless to expect the emerging nations to establish institutions exactly like those which have functioned in the very different conditions of advanced industrial nations. In the contest for the minds of the uncommitted nations in which we are now engaged, it will be of crucial importance for the West to show enough imaginative understanding so that these inevitable differences will not prevent the growth of partnership. The test for such partnership therefore cannot be whether the other nation has already organised itself on democratic lines but whether such a development is still open to it, and is being seriously pursued. The co-operation which is now needed is not simply a matter of providing and accepting aid but of developing a sense of solidarity. The free nations, bound together for a common purpose, should find this much easier to achieve than the Communist bloc whose very system is based on the denial of free partnership.

W.B.

July, 1957

I

DEMOCRATIC INSTITUTIONS

IN

WESTERN EUROPE

I

DEMOCRATIC INSTITUTIONS IN WESTERN EUROPE

WERNER BURMEISTER

THREE new republics emerged from the ruins of the second Great War in Western Europe.[1] In a world devoted to gloom and fear, their achievements in rebuilding democratic institutions present quite a heartening story. They were deeply divided from one another and within themselves by historical experience, traditional enmities and recent wrongs. In France and Italy, the leaders of powerful Communist parties were members of the new governments until 1947, a year which was to prove a great turning point in Europe. Their claim to a share in governmental responsibility had been securely established during the Resistance period and in accordance with their doctrines they expected that, in due course, they would achieve absolute power. In Germany, a Communist regime was set up by the Red Army in the Soviet zone of occupation, and almost at once it became clear that the Soviet rulers were determined to exact acceptance of a Communist regime in the whole of Germany as the price of reunification, a determination which twelve years later remained completely unaffected by changes in Soviet leadership.

In a society where democratic institutions are to function successfully, there must be some measure of agreement on basic principles beneath and beyond all party disputes. In the absence of such basic unity, the chances seemed small in 1945 that any of these three democracies would be able to survive their infancy. Observers in older democracies sometimes forget how gradual the process was by which they established their own institutions and how greatly they were favoured not merely by good manage-

---

[1] It would be presumptuous to try to discuss the whole of Western Europe in a single paper. This survey therefore has to be confined to the three principal continental states of Western Europe, Germany, France and Italy.

3

ment but also by good luck. Decent and capable rulers, a sense
of historical achievement, reasonable prosperity, some geographical security from external aggression have all played their part.
So, of course, has the ability to learn from history. Writing in
1927, Balfour argued (in his preface to Walter Bagehot's
English Constitution) that 'our whole political machinery pre-
supposes a people so fundamentally at one that they can safely
afford to bicker; and so sure of their own moderation that they
are not dangerously disturbed by the never-ending din of political
conflict.' This was written soon after the General Strike which
had profoundly shaken the British political fabric. And the
most important feature of that experience was not that it seemed
to bring Britain to the brink of civil war, but that both sides
seem to have been determined ever since to avoid the recurrence
of a similar situation.

Since modern democratic institutions owe so much to British
developments, it may be useful to remind ourselves that British
people on the whole are not prone to overestimate the formative
influence of institutions, as distinct from the influence of the men
who serve in them. It is true that in their public life they
rightly insist on certain modes of behaviour likely to induce
restraint, self-discipline and a certain degree of outward conformity. They cultivate and expect humour, in the sense of
both good temper and that imaginative faculty which helps us
to laugh together. All this greatly assists in the orderly and
peaceful conduct of political disputes. But they are not much
given to the error that democratic institutions produce democrats,
though they may produce conditions in which democrats can
grow.

In fact, democratic institutions pre-suppose the existence of
at least some democrats since they cannot long function without
them. There must be a desire for freedom and for the active
exercise of freedom, coupled with a sense of social responsibility.
Above all, there must be a minimum of mutual confidence
between the citizens of a free state. Without it, they cannot
freely co-operate. (Hence those aspiring to be dictators must
always seek to destroy mutual confidence and to replace it by

mutual fear. In the absolute state co-operation must be the result of coercion so that it can be completely controlled. It is then called 'spontaneous.') One aspect of co-operation in a free society is the readiness of its citizens not merely to share in making the law but also in upholding it and not to rely for this purpose exclusively upon the police and the courts. They must have a sense of partnership with their neighbours and a sense of independence towards authority. Although this is certainly never true of all the members of a free society, these qualities must be present in an adequate number of them—adequate, that is, to determine the political climate. The ability to form large political parties is perhaps another of these indispensable qualities, at any rate in large societies. Large parties, if they are to hold together, must be tolerant. They cannot afford narrow doctrines or the advocacy of narrow interests. By diminishing political sectarianism, they help to create conditions of political stability.

Observers on the Continent of Europe are inclined to think that the presence of these qualities in Britain is due to something called the British tradition. But traditions are not bestowed from on high, like manna from Heaven. They are usually the result of conscious or instinctive choice, and they are maintained by deliberate purpose. In some ways, however, Continental observers are right. Britain has had advantages, right up to 1945, which were absent over large parts of Europe. One of the most striking differences is of course to be found in the field of political institutions. In Britain, changes in the traditional forms of political life have all been gradual; they have been carried out in response to popular demand or at least with popular consent. The experience of Continental Europe has been radically different. There, during the last quarter of a century, constitutions, institutions and customary ways of life have been shattered by *coup d'états,* wars, revolutions and military occupations. National unity, often relatively new and tenuous, was replaced by deep divisions, moderation by fanaticism and mutual hatred, fanaticism by apathy or cynicism. That process had begun well before the outbreak of war in 1939. The war cemented national unity in Britain; it left her constitution intact and her territory inviolate. Exactly the opposite happened in Italy, France and Germany, to take the three states with which we are here concerned. The war that was waged over their territories left these nations deeply divided in their loyalties. In France and Italy it left behind vastly enlarged Communist parties with their allegiance directed towards a foreign power and prepared virtually to 'contract out' of their own state if they could not conquer it. In all three countries, the new governments did not merely have to re-establish democratic institutions but also the physical basis of existence, industry, transport and communications, agriculture and housing. The two tasks had to be solved simultaneously. All historical experience shows that without prosperity, or hope of prosperity, democracy cannot function.

Marshall Aid, the European Recovery Programme and the various programmes of interim aid that preceded it, did not merely help to surmount the crippling difficulties of the first few years of hand-to-mouth existence. It also helped to create the basis for wider co-operation. That process was also aided by the emergence of similar political parties in the three countries —the Christian Democrats in Italy and Germany, the M.R.P. in France—all destined to play a decisive role in their respective governments. Churches are among the few institutions which survive dictatorships, and the Christian ethic seemed to have gathered new strength from terror and persecution. It was therefore easier for Roman Catholics than for almost any other group to form once again their own political parties. In Western Germany, the Christian Democrats from the very start sought to attract Protestants into the ranks of their party, but they achieved their initial success primarily among the Roman Catholic population whose numbers and proportion had been vastly increased by the expulsion of Germans from Eastern Europe and by the division of Germany. A predominantly Protestant population remained under Soviet rule in Eastern Germany.

But the new democracies also entered into a legacy of social and economic problems which had persisted quite apart from the war. In Italy it was overpopulation and the disparity between the industrial north and the agricultural south. France had been suffering from economic stagnation and, like Italy, from extreme unevenness in the distribution of wealth and income. In both countries, reforms had been obstructed by those who would lose, or thought they would lose, their privileged position. Even after 1945, their influence and resources enabled them to exercise sufficient pressure on the political parties of the middle class to prevent basic changes. Their opposition could, and still can, bring down governments. More than one Italian government has come to grief on the problem of land reform, while in France the forces of *immobilism* confined most governments, at least up to 1953, to the maintenance of a synthetic stability by means of high tariffs, subsidies and budget deficits. French economic expansion since 1953 seemed to pave the way towards social readjustments, but its effects have unfortunately been cancelled out by the ever growing burdens of the conflict in Algeria.

In Western Germany, some concessions have been made to the demand for industrial democracy put forward by the united trade union movement which emerged after the war and which, for the first time in German history, organised both Socialist and Christian (*i.e.*, mainly Roman Catholic) workers in the same streamlined industrial unions. 'Co-determination,' although it did not fulfil the early hopes attached to it, gave some share in the control of basic industries to workers' representatives. But more important than this was the rapid economic recovery of the country. Although its material rewards were very unequally distributed and greatly favoured the controllers of industry and commerce, the expansion was so swift and general that its benefits soon began to spread downwards to wage and salary earners. The tendency for living standards to rise is often of greater social and political significance than the actual level reached. Not much was heard of the demand for fair shares. The awareness of industrial and black-coated workers in Germany that they were somewhat better off this year than last, and that this improvement was likely to continue, made them willing to tolerate undoubted social inequalities and thus contributed to industrial and political stability. During the early years of industrial reconstruction, strikes would in any case have been doubtful weapons, so long as there was a large reserve of unemployed labour from among those millions of German expellees and refugees who had come from Eastern Europe or from Germany's former eastern territories. The rapid absorption of this industrial reserve army made it possible to create new records of production and at the same time deprived political extremists of a splendid opportunity.

Germans have objected to the term 'economic miracle' which has been applied to their performance since the currency reform of 1948. They insist that it was hard work and not magic that enabled them to rise from the pit of poverty to unprecedented prosperity. One of the reasons for the sustained energy they have shown in this field is perhaps to be found in their recent political history. Most nations, when they reflect on their performance, prefer to have a sense of achievement. Germans, if they did so, could only experience a sense of disastrous failure. After the end of the war, they could only hope to rise again by a supreme effort. And that effort enabled them to escape from historical reflection into economic pursuits. Prosperity could, and did, provide a sense of both national and individual achievement. In some of its aspects, therefore, it was a case of justification by works. The effort involved has been highly competitive. It has produced a hard-faced society whose members are not much inclined to show charity towards one another, perhaps rather less so the higher they are in the social scale. This does not mean that there is not adequate provision for the sick, the old or the needy. On the contrary, social welfare has been steadily improved. But those in need of help have to rely almost exclusively on public authority. The spirit of neighbourly help, so beneficial in itself and so essential for democracy, is not greatly in evidence.

Both France and Italy show similar features, and perhaps the spirit of active kindness tends to decline in all countries where social welfare must necessarily become more and more a function of the State. In Italy, the situation is made worse by large scale and persistent unemployment, particularly in the south, and by the general poverty of a country with few natural resources. An unemployment figure of nearly two million has become an almost traditional feature of the Italian economy. The vast majority of these consists of unskilled labour. The disappointing results of the agreement for the transfer of Italian workers to Federal Germany appear to have been primarily due to the fact that Germany wanted skilled workers.

There are of course historical reasons as well for this weakness of the sense of social responsibility. In France, feudalism was replaced by a highly individualist order which strictly divides the public and the private spheres of life. This has left an indelible imprint on the attitude of Frenchmen to State and society. They often appear as abstract notions, to be treated with reserve or even hostility. Over large parts of continental Europe, including Germany and Italy, feudalism remained a powerful political factor right up to the second Great War. There is no space here to discuss the reasons for its survival or for the extraordinary degree of influence exercised by its representatives quite out of proportion to their number and significance. Some of them certainly had a sense of public service and of social obligation, but the politically decisive section seemed concerned only to preserve their privileges. They rarely experienced any difficulty in persuading themselves that their own vested interests were identical with those of their nations. They always were overwhelmingly on the side of reaction. And whereas in Britain, during the nineteenth century, the representatives of the new middle classes gradually imposed their views and standards upon society as a whole, almost the opposite happened in countries like Germany and Italy where the new captains of industry often tended to adopt the outlook and political attitudes of this older ruling class. The effects were probably more far reaching in Germany because of the predominant influence wielded by Prussia in shaping the new Reich and its society. And in Prussia the firmly established Junker nobility and the efficient bureaucracy continued to reinforce one another. Here the new industrial classes, capitalists and workers, met a pre-established order capable of imposing its pre-industrial standards to an extent unthinkable in nineteenth century England. Thus the political institutions of imperial Germany were quite out of harmony with its social reality. This disharmony which constantly grew worse helped to precipitate the nation into the war of 1914 and the half-hearted revolution of 1918.

Neither in Germany nor in Italy did the middle classes develop the same sense of independence and of leadership as they did in Britain. They never managed to make themselves the undisputed masters of the machinery of state. And so they were not able to present the emerging working class with a practical example of political emancipation by legal and constitutional means. It is no accident that Marxism acquired no hold in the country where it was conceived; or that the German working class movement adopted its doctrines during the period of Bismarckian repression; or that Italy today has a large Communist party. For in Britain, the working class and its political representatives quite naturally came to look upon themselves as part of a nation which conducts its own affairs. In Germany, on the other hand, they considered themselves excluded from 'the State' right up to 1918, while the Kaiser and his advisers had tried to exclude them even from the nation. They were given little chance of acquiring the art of governing the nation until political power suddenly dropped into their lap because the old autocratic State had collapsed under the blows of crushing military defeat. Even then, as the fate of Germany and Italy between the two wars was to show, the power of the older political forces was not finally broken. In both countries, middle class and working class representatives continued to feel uncertain and insecure in the exercise of political power until it was taken from them, almost without a struggle, by dictators who had rallied the forces of discontent with the encouragement and backing of these older social classes. Their support at this juncture was no less momentous than the contributions which industrialists made to the party funds of the dictators.

It is true that many Prussian Junker families were honourably represented among those who tried to overthrow the Nazi regime in 1944 and who subsequently paid for their failure with their lives. But whatever were the reasons for this failure, historically and politically the attempt came too late. In a sense, these men died—as millions of others did—in part, at least, because their fathers had tried to turn back the wheels of history and, in doing so, had not hesitated to condone murder as an instrument of policy. And now murder had become the only instrument of policy. Without the physical destruction of Hitler, no change of policy could even be attempted. If he escaped assassination, the gamble on which he had staked the whole existence of the nation which he pretended to love would have to be continued to the bitter end. If those who were executed by Hitler's orders did in fact represent a new departure in German politics, they were tragically unable to prove their ideas. Hitler exterminated them, and the Red Army completed their destruction by annexing their historical territory, by dividing their domains and by installing there the very regime against which the Junkers had always proclaimed themselves as a bulwark. It seems more than doubtful whether they can ever reconstitute themselves as a social—or military—class.

In Italy the contest continues. The fate of the country's democratic institutions is bound up with the continuation of land reform and the integration of the working class into the new State. In a society with deep-seated sources of social discontent, extremism cannot be overcome simply by invoking the superior values, moral and political, of parliamentary government. They have to be demonstrated in action. Presumably the vast majority of those who vote for Communist candidates in Italy—and in France—are not doing so because of a deep attachment to the principles of dialectical materialism but because they wish to protest against the conditions under which they live. Economic and social reform must therefore remain the most decisive method of reducing Communist influence. Nobody is more aware of this than the Communist leaders themselves. Hence they try to sabotage reforms, or to claim credit for them if they cannot prevent them. They are not primarily interested in removing social evils but in achieving power. A sense of all-pervading and deepening crisis is therefore a condition of their ultimate success.

Naturally, there are other factors involved. Anti-clericalism is one of them. In a Roman Catholic country, a political movement whose leaders claim to possess an equally authoritative dogma, but one that can be translated into reality here and now if only they are given power, clearly has great attraction for those who wish to fight the influence of priests without losing the benefit of an all-embracing faith. But it would seem that this widespread desire for a substitute religion in the guise of a political creed arises precisely when individuals feel helpless in the face of social reality, or when they are unable to interpret for themselves the complexities of their situation and therefore wish to shift the awful burden of thought. Here, then, is an additional reason why the value of democratic institutions must be proved not merely in intellectual argument but in practical achievement.

The relative instability of governments in France and Italy, compared with Federal Germany, is not, of course, simply due to the strength of the Communist parties in the former two and its complete disappearance as a parliamentary group in Western Germany. French and Italian governments have been constantly faced with two oppositions, the Communists and the right-wing political parties. Both of these can unite to bring their parliaments into disrepute and to overthrow their governments, but they are unable to form a new one. However slender and insecure the parliamentary majority of the centre parties might be, they are kept in power because no alternative majority exists. This frequently forces them to compromise their political principles since a withdrawal from governmental responsibility might involve the end of parliamentary government itself. This has been particularly true in France where governments now seem to owe their survival to the law of inertia, and where the Radicals —the most typical of French political parties and perhaps of liberal parties everywhere—have tried to be simultaneously both in the government and in the opposition. In Italy, too, the reunification of the Saragat Social Democrats with the Nenni Socialists could weaken parliamentary government if it forced the united Socialist party into more or less permanent opposition.

The German Federal Republic has so far been spared these embarrassments. Its Founding Fathers, recalling the experiences of the Weimar Republic when Nazis and Communists joined forces in order to hasten the end of democracy, incorporated into the new Constitution the ingenious device of the 'constructive vote of no confidence.' This means that a chancellor (and his cabinet) can only be removed from office if the Bundestag elects a new chancellor in his place. There is no other constitutional method of changing the government. Normally, therefore, only a split in the cabinet, or in the governing majority party or coalition, can bring down a government. Whether this device would be of real value in preserving parliamentary government during a prolonged constitutional crisis bitterly dividing the nation must be open to doubt. Such a situation has not yet arisen. Dr. Adenauer's coalition government has always enjoyed a safe majority, and in 1953 his own political party, the Christian Democrats, achieved an absolute majority over all other parties. Equally important, however, for German political stability has been the existence of the Social Democrats as a responsible and united opposition party, strong enough to form the basis of an alternative government. Moreover, not all the centre parties were needed, as in France, to provide a governmental majority. The Free Democrats were able to break away from the coalition without endangering Dr. Adenauer's government. One of their reasons for doing so was the wish to obtain the best conditions for joining, as a minority party, either the Social Democrats or the Christian Democrats after the general election of September 1957, in the hope, presumably, that either of these two large parties would then need their support in order to form the next government. By and large, the Free Democrats agree with the government on an economic policy favouring free enterprise and with the Social Democrats in their critical attitude towards Dr. Adenauer's foreign policy. The election programme of the Social Democrats, with its insistence on respect for private property and freedom of competition, would certainly seem to facilitate a realignment, even though the leader of the Free Democrats still professes to fear that 'the Social Democrats might be overwhelmed by the Socialists within their party.'

One of the significant political features of the Federal Republic is therefore that two moderate political parties now face each other as respective leaders of government and opposition. The voters, moreover, seem increasingly to approve of this arrangement. At practically every election during recent years a growing proportion of votes has been cast for these two parties at the expense of the smaller ones. This tendency has probably been strengthened by the fact that Germans seem to have developed a greater interest in increased consumption than in ideological perfection. Such an attitude favours the formation of large political parties, as it has done in Britain and the United States. It is a cumulative process since it places either party within reach of undivided political power, at least for the duration of a single parliament, and thereby induces both of them to tolerate different shades of opinion within their own ranks and to woo the uncommitted voter. He may or may not be 'floating,' but his support is needed for an overall majority. No party narrowly representing a sectional interest can normally hope to achieve such a position. And since most of the uncommitted voters are likely to be found somewhere near the middle of the road, particularly among the growing ranks of the 'salariat,' party programmes come to look more and more alike. Ideologies are gradually dismantled or become attenuated by the sheer passage of time. The Christian Democrats are turned into a secularised conservative party; and the Social Democrats, having discarded Marx, become a party of social reform. Differences between them are increasingly those of degree and emphasis.

This tendency is partly concealed in Germany by conflicts over foreign policy and defence. To some extent, it is probably just the absence of deep-seated disagreement on domestic matters which is responsible for shifting the opposition's attack into this other field. There is also a feeling of frustration among Social Democrats at their continued exclusion from power at the federal

level, even though they have at all times shared power and
responsibility in some of the Länder governments. Moreover,
the Social Democrats have consistently tended to overestimate
the freedom of manœuvre that exists nowadays in matters of
foreign policy, particularly in relations with Russia. The
deplorable lack of consultation between government and opposition probably provides an added reason for their bitter criticism
of Dr. Adenauer. It is a serious weakness of the German
political system that it has not been possible so far to establish
the indispensable minimum of mutual confidence between those
who exercise governmental power and those who hope to do so
one day. Politics is not merely a matter of institutions but also
of human relations. In this field, the initiative must rest with the
government of the day.

The Germans have not fought for their democratic institutions; they have merely settled down to them. Consequently,
they may not feel deeply involved in defending them. Nevertheless, this process has had some important political results.
One, as we have seen already, is the establishment, for the first
time in German history, of a conservative party which accepts
the principles of parliamentary government. Conservatives
under the Kaiser believed that the best method of dealing with
the Reichstag was to order 'one lieutenant and ten men' to send
it packing. Their successors in the Weimar Republic helped
Hitler into power. Democracy was destroyed with the active and
enthusiastic support of large sections of the upper and middle
classes. At that stage, the Social Democrats were in fact the
only democratic element in the Weimar Republic, too irresolute
and too weak numerically to sustain it. The Federal Republic,
on the other hand, is largely a middle class creation. Almost
symbolically, its first President is a university professor and its
first Chancellor a former burgomaster, although an exceptional
one. Naturally, not all the former Nazis are dead or converts
to democracy. Many have simply adopted a protective colour-
ing, have gone into industry or trade or have found a quiet niche
in the civil service. Those who still have political ambitions
gravitate instinctively towards sources of discontent, towards

nationalist aspirations or refugee organisations. All this is not surprising. What seems more significant is that, so far, they have seen so little opportunity of showing their hand. The secret of political stability seems to have been the concurrence of rising prosperity with the establishment of a strong executive based on a parliament by no means docile but composed of large and moderate political groups.

Historical experience has made the strong executive more suspect in France than in Germany. In France, political divisions are too deep and too numerous for a strong government to be formed, except by imposition. The instability of cabinets is considered less disturbing than the danger of autocratic government. Figures like de Gaulle and Poujade seem to be reminders that the authoritarian tradition is still alive. But its exponents must now appeal increasingly to the grievances of the small man, and a mass movement of resentful shopkeepers is neither an inspiring spectacle nor convincing as a force of political regeneration. This may have been one of the reasons for de Gaulle's hesitancy and eventual failure. André Malraux has complained that ‘ de Gaulle marched us full speed to the Rubicon—and then told us to get out our fishing rods,’ but perhaps de Gaulle had come to the conclusion that fishing rods was what they really wanted.

Until quite recently, moreover, most Frenchmen seemed to feel that the political instability was more apparent than real. The administrative machinery of the country continues to work smoothly enough even while there is a cabinet crisis. Even more striking is the fact that more or less the same people who were members of the last government will be found again in the new one, though perhaps in a different post. The only prime minister of the post-war period who tried to achieve some basic reforms, M. Mendès-France, passionately protested against this feature of French political life and claimed that it was contrary to the will of France that adversity should cement these statues into their pedestals. But it is difficult to be dogmatic about the will of France, and perhaps the simile was not well chosen either. Changes of French governments rather tend to resemble a game of musical chairs, and when the music stopped after M. Mendès-France had spoken, he found himself without a chair.

Since the stability of democratic institutions depends above all on the strength of the moderate political parties, it is not surprising that attempts have repeatedly been made, both in France and Italy, to remedy the numerical weakness of those parties by means of changing the electoral law. Proposals of this kind are usually centred on the idea that only the moderate parties can enter into electoral pacts with one another, whereas the Communists and the right wing opposition are not normally able to join forces for election purposes. If, therefore, proportional representation could be so modified that any party or alliance of parties polling a majority of votes in a group of constituencies would get either all the seats in that area or a bonus of seats, the moderates would be able to secure a comfortable majority in parliament. This method, which Herbert Lüthy has described as 'rescuing the Republic from the people by means of arithmetic,' has been tried in Italy in 1953 where it narrowly failed to achieve the desired result because the alliance of centre parties obtained only 49.85 per cent of the valid votes cast. A similar plan in the Federal Republic, which would have favoured the Christian Democrats, had to be abandoned, largely because the smaller parties threatened to bring about a realignment in some of the Länder governments. The representatives of the Länder in the second chamber (Bundesrat) would then have been able to block the proposal there.

While party advantage is of course an important motive in all such plans for electoral reform, there is also the desire to secure under proportional representation some of the benefits of the majority system or of single-member constituencies, particularly the reduction it produces in the number of political parties. Their multiplicity has often threatened to bring parliamentary government to a complete standstill, apart from bringing it into disrepute. The view seems to be gaining ground that it is not the purpose of parliaments to reflect with mathematical exactitude the political divisions among the electorate but to create the basis for stable representative government. Moreover, under proportional representation, the voter can rarely foresee the composition and programme of the government which will emerge since these questions can only be settled after the election. It is only when the various political parties know their relative strength that they can begin to negotiate with one another about the formation of a coalition government. Even then the programme of the government may not be decided by its own members but by the parties behind it who may threaten to withdraw 'their ministers' if they do not like the government's policy. It is in fact government by remote control. Responsibilities for success or failure are bound to get blurred. In a two-party contest, on the other hand, each of the parties can present its programme beforehand, and the voter will be in a better position to judge their relative merits before he decides once more which of them should be entrusted with the government. There is also the argument that in single-member constituencies the result is influenced by the personal qualities of candidates, but the extent of that influence may sometimes be overestimated by outside observers.

A modified form of proportional representation continues to be used in the Federal Republic, with provisions designed to eliminate parties obtaining less than 5 per cent of the total number of votes cast. (There are additional provisions for first and second preferences, direct and indirect election, etc., which need not detain us here.) In 1953, Christian Democrats and Social Democrats together attracted over 70 per cent of all the votes. The Communist party obtained just over 2 per cent and had virtually disappeared as a political force before it was banned by a decision of the Constitutional Court in 1956. The ban was in fact widely criticised in Germany as being unnecessary. The proximity of the Soviet system, knowledge of conditions in the Soviet zone of occupation, and the continued division of the country all combined to impair the attractiveness of the Communist party. A small neo-Nazi party was similarly banned by the Court. The absence of a Nazi revival has been a real handicap to the Communists. These two extremist groups need each other so as to be able to sell 'protection.'

The Communist parties of France and Italy have been placed on the defence by developments in the Soviet Union and in Eastern Europe, particularly in Poland and Hungary. They are still strong and well organised and continue to exercise a powerful influence through Communist-controlled trade union organisations. But they have lost much of their drive and appeal, and they have no early prospect of gaining power. This should enable the three Western European states to continue the consolidation of their democratic institutions. The first phase of development after the war was undoubtedly—and perhaps inevitably—dominated by the desire for the restoration of older and familiar forms of social and political life. Sometimes this hankering after those older patterns which preceded the war and the pre-war crisis came to look like a thoroughly retrograde development and, in some way, this impression was justified. France returned from the Fourth to the Third Republic, Italy to clericalism, Germany to paternalism. But only a superficial observer could persuade himself that this was the whole of the story. The period of restoration was probably essential if the nations concerned were to get back sufficient health and strength to enable them to take the next step. And if the first step had to be the restoration of their economic and political apparatus, the next step must be the reform and renewal of their societies and its institutions. It might have been better if the two processes could have gone hand in hand to a larger extent than they did. However, remembering the intolerably frequent changes in their fate and institutions during the lifetime of one generation, most Frenchmen, Italians, Germans probably welcomed a pause. At any rate, the conditions of reform have now been created; there is a growing awareness of the need for reform in all three countries; and there are signs that the second phase has already started. In Italy, the development of the South and the problem of land reform have been tackled; the supporters of social reform among the Christian Democrats appear to be still in the ascendancy; and the split in the Socialist party might be healed with a consequent gain for the forces of democracy. In Germany rising prosperity—and perhaps the prospect of the 1957 general election—have facilitated social legislation which is now being studied by the Government and the Opposition in Britain. The prospects are perhaps more problematical in France where there is so much resignation and where the chances of reform are tied up with the solution of the Algerian problem. It is hardly necessary to add that this next move forward can only come if there is no military conflict in Europe and no major economic crisis.

It is equally important that the three countries and their Western European neighbours should sustain the development of co-operation beyond military defence into the political, social and economic fields. It was both natural and sensible for this co-operation to start on a functional basis, in matters of coal and steel, of payments, of a common market. But ultimately there will be a need 'to form a more perfect union' or, at any rate, to create a wider harmony, not in order to obliterate differences in character, temper and outlook, but in order to protect them. The progress made in promoting the solidarity of Western Europe seems to show awareness of the fact that the old national sovereign State is no longer equal to the tasks and techniques of our time. Modern democracy arose in Europe together with nationalism. It nearly died of that alliance, as Lord Acton foresaw when he wrote (in 1862) that 'nationality does not aim either at liberty or prosperity, both of which it sacrifices to the imperative need of making the nation the mould and measure of the State.' In all three countries, democratic institutions have been destroyed at one time or another in order to promote aggressive policies: in France by Napoleon; in Italy by Mussolini; in Germany by Hitler. If basic unity and moderation are the prerequisite of democracy within each country, these qualities have now become equally indispensable for the relationship between free countries.

II
DEMOCRATIC INSTITUTIONS
IN THE
UNITED STATES OF AMERICA

II

DEMOCRATIC INSTITUTIONS IN THE UNITED STATES OF AMERICA

RICHARD H. PEAR

THE political institutions of a democratic country are only a part, though an important part, of the total culture of its people. They are an important part, for it is through them that the aspirations and values of a people find some of their expression, and it is in them, particularly in the judiciary, that fundamental political values from time to time find as accurate expression as is possible, given the approximate nature of most political and constitutional language. Beneath the visible peak of discussion and adjudication according to law, lie the mass of human beings organised into groups, institutions, regional and economic sections, religious and cultural associations, families and neighbourhood units. The light of publicity shines continually on the peak and the moves of the personalities and policies up there are the object of professional description, analysis and criticism, varying from the technical analyses of the law journals to the headlines of the tabloid press. Below the peak, sociological studies, 'test case' analyses of political processes, and the old-fashioned politician and journalist who live with their ears close to the ground, provide us with more or less accurate information on the meaning of the confused rumblings of ordinary peoples' ideas and hopes.

To relate the formalised concepts of the constitutional law, the avowed political policies of identifiable political leaders, the solemn pronouncements of national business, labour and farm organisations to the actual life of the people, calls for great knowledge and literary skill. Fortunately for the foreign student, America with its well-known dislike of sacred cows and state secrets has trained generations of journalists to relate the facts of ordinary life to the principles of the constitution, and what is at least as important, the principles of the constitution to the facts of life. While Mr. Dave Beck in Washington D.C. claims the protection of the Fifth Amendment when a congressional committee endeavours to probe into his leadership of the Teamsters Union, a local newspaper man in Seattle explains some of the background which gave rise to Mr. Beck's difficulties —and gets a Pulitzer prize for his journalism.

Chief Justice John Marshall early in the nineteenth century warned his fellow lawyers to remember that it was a *constitution* that they were expounding, an instrument of government designed to endure for ages to come. This was a highly significant dictum, the implications of which have, fortunately, been well understood by most subsequent Supreme Courts; and the manner in which Supreme Court justices are appointed (*i.e.*, by the President) has prevented the legal fraternity from expecting that decisions will always be technically correct and bound to precedents whatever the possible consequences. The possible consequences are always in the mind of the Supreme Court, and the search is frequently for a decision which will prove to be both possible, acceptable administratively, and in accord with the general direction of public opinion. It has not always been so, but for twenty years the court has tried not to isolate itself from the trends of public life, not to invalidate legislation passed by the Federal Congress and not to be drawn into enunciating new constitutional principles. It is not always possible to satisfy the whole country : it is not always possible to avoid the declaration of new constitutional principle. This is well illustrated by the controversy over the court's anti-segregation ruling of 1954. The North regards it as being in accord with current feeling in America and in a logical line with certain recent court decisions in the field of university education. The South regards it as a 'sociological' decision, and in flagrant breach of some strictly 'legal' decisions which have upheld 'separate but equal' treatment for Negroes in primary education. And, of course, the South is right, except for the fact that the *Plessy* decision of 1896 upholding segregation was no more legal or less 'sociological' than the 1954 decision which reversed it. Even in its

striking decisions of June 1957 affecting the rights of those con-
victed on evidence from F.B.I. agents (the whole of which was
not available to the defence) the Supreme Court is not enunciating new doctrine. It is returning to a position which was always
that of a powerful dissenting minority in the court : it is respond-
ing to the waning of McCarthyism, and it has *not* invalidated
the Smith Act—however difficult it has now made it to get
convictions of Communists under that Act.

The main point of this examination of the position of the
court is to emphasise that in the United States there is today
no significant tendency to claim priority for the 'pays légal'
over the 'pays réel,' or even to draw a thick line between them.
Lawyers write about the law, political scientists and journalists
describe and criticise political and legal procedures, and each
writer has an audience ; but not even in the United States with
its vast numbers of lawyers, politicians and social scientists are
all the people interested in the social sciences all the time. Nor
for that matter are all Americans interested in their revered
political institutions all the time. The Frenchman with his much
criticised political institutions and his seeming indifference to
the fate of his central government is a much more dedicated
voter than the American. What we have to understand therefore
if we wish to get a country's political institutions into perspective,
is not merely what they are and how they work, but whether
the people themselves see them as the writers do, whether they
feel that they are good institutions (and why they feel that way),
what frustrations they create in the attitudes of ordinary men
and women, and whether these frustrations or irritations find out-
lets in the form of other quasi-political or social organisations.

This warning is particularly necessary for a foreign student
of American affairs, for in a formal constitutional sense American
institutions have hardly changed at all since the Constitution was
adopted at the end of the eighteenth century. By a usage—not
an amendment—which is now over a century old—the President
is, in fact, elected in a way the Founding Fathers did not foresee : by the 11th Amendment the Vice-President is chosen in a
different manner ; the Senate is, by the 17th Amendment, elected

now by a popular vote in the States : and the 22nd Amendment
—the most recent—limits the President to two terms of office
only.   But the original Constitution embodying an elected Chief
Executive, a Lower House representing the States according to
population, an Upper House (in which, irrespective of population, each state has two Senators), and an appointed Supreme
Court—all these still stand as they did in the days of George
Washington, when the American population was creeping up to
four million, most of whom were engaged in agriculture.   Today
the population of the U.S.A. is moving on to the 170 million
mark, and the vast majority are connected with industry and
commerce, not agriculture;   America, contrary to the advice
of Washington and Jefferson is actively engaged in pursuing
foreign politics on a world scale, is making binding alliances and,
if Formosa is a portent, is beginning to experience the normal
difficulties of great powers who extend their protection to their
less advanced brothers across the seas.

   The next question to which we must turn is to explain how
it is that America's political institutions remain unchanged—
and then to query the assertion that they are in fact unchanged.
Formally, the institutions are essentially as they were in the beginning.   America has by far the oldest, and most successful written
constitution in the world.   Why has it been unnecessary to change
the political institutions of the American constitution?   Here
we can only sketch out possible answers to this question.   We
can, in passing, note the argument that the Constitution stands
as a rock because the Founding Fathers were endowed with a
political wisdom and foresight never before vouchsafed to any
other group of mortals.   Looking at the Founding Fathers one
by one, they were interesting, energetic, sensible and patriotic
men, who knew that the old constitution (the Articles of Con-
federation) was an unsatisfactory instrument of government, and
who wished to devise an improved instrument and knew, in a
general way, what improvements were desirable.   They argued
and compromised and left much unsaid.   These compromises
proved effective, and their unsaid pieces were filled in later by
politicians, judges and events.

One can claim for them great wisdom or great good fortune, but to be fair to them, there were two important characteristics of the Founding Fathers which deserve mention. The American Revolution was something of an ideological struggle—at least Tom Paine tried to make it so—and the Declaration of Independence was a document full of high principles of political philosophy. The Founding Fathers were neither ideologues nor political theorists; nor for that matter were most of them democrats. But as intelligent conservatives and men of affairs, they realised that the people ought to have some voice in government policy—not because the people were right in their political judgments, but because to deny them a voice would be asking for trouble. So they gave them that voice in the Lower House. The states had feelings of statehood and some claim to sovereignty in domestic affairs, so they gave them equality in the Upper House and (by the 10th Amendment, 1791) the right to legislate in their areas on any matters not specifically declared to be federal matters by the U.S. constitution nor denied by that constitution to the states. They separated the legislature of the central government from the Executive lest the former should make the latter its creature, and arranged for the election of the Executive in a manner which, if not democratic, was at least representative of the better elements in the nation : and they gave the Executive some important powers to exercise either on its own or with the consent of the Senate. The Supreme Court was set up to adjudicate between state and state and between states and the Federal government. ' Judicial review' by the court of federal legislation was a logical development as long as the Constitution declared that it (the Constitution) was the supreme law of the land, but whether this was anticipated or intended by the Founding Fathers is still in debate. Secondly, it has been emphasised that what was important about the Philadelphia Convention was the things upon which it did not legislate. It left the question of the suffrage to the states; it left the state form of government to be decided by the states, provided that they were 'republican' forms : it left slavery where it was, although it arranged a date after which importation of slaves would cease : it left religion and education, the question of a free press and freedom of assembly to be handled by the states—although it did say that freedom of the press, of speech, of assembly and of religion could not be abridged by *Federal* law.   In letting well alone in so many spheres of human activity the authors of the Constitution seem to have shown great wisdom and the true conservative instinct for minimising the role of formal politics and administration.   Finally, but of some importance, the Constitution was written in clear and attractive language and was, as these things go, admirably short.   As a medium of popular and patriotic education it has been unrivalled.

Disputes at once arose between the Federalist Party and the Jeffersonian Republicans (later to be called Democrats) as to the interpretation of the Constitution, particularly the clauses granting powers to the Federal government.   The disputes were sometimes bitter, but it was perhaps an advantage (from the point of view of the viability of the new Constitution) that its clear and simple words *could* be interpreted in different ways and that constitutional issues became political issues.   Both parties claimed guardianship of the Constitution, and however much they disputed over its meaning, the very fact that they purported to defend it from its enemies meant that in the popular mind it must have appeared worth defending.   If one side had wanted to keep it and the other to abolish it matters would have been different.   Even in that dramatic and bloody constitutional tragedy—the Civil War—the Constitution itself escaped largely unscathed.   This was the supreme test, and the proof of the toughness of the constitutional idea is to be found not only in the South's acceptance of the abolition, by constitutional amendment, of slavery and involuntary servitude, but even more in the fact that, even in the South, there has never been any serious move subsequently to abolish the old Constitution and create another.

Politics in the United States is often about the Constitution, but it is about its 'possession' by one party or its interpretation by a politically appointed court, not about its very existence. In fact it now looks as if the politicians realised far earlier than did the constitutional writers that it could be used for a variety of desirable political ends. But it remains a quite remarkable fact nevertheless that no substantial body of persons has ever wanted to alter it radically or abolish it. The existence of a very difficult process of amendment, which in other countries might have encouraged root and branch opposition, only, it seems, adds to its unique position in the world.

From a comparison with the life and politics of other lands, American historians are now endeavouring to find new and non-political reasons for the stability of political institutions in the U.S.A. Until recently it was conventional to attribute the successes of the U.S.A. to two main factors. Firstly that in the beginning they were endowed with an almost perfect democratic political constitution : and secondly, that the American people being nurtured in the true spirit of democratic values by their reverence for that constitution, developed that sturdy individualism which as a general rule of economics and sociology *must* (it was believed) lead to personal happiness, economic success and a law-abiding and patriotic citizenry. Considering this as a general proposition modern scholars have looked at other countries. They find, even in the U.S., no correlation between individualism and obedience to the law ; in other countries, little significant relationship between democratic constitutions and individual economic success and, in their own and other countries, a doubtful equation of economic success and personal happiness as defined and measured by modern psychological tests. Worse still for the ethical bases of the American success story, they have discovered as much, or more, evidence of social co-operation than of aggressive individualism in the history of the American frontier. In addition they are beset by the theories of Prof. Wright Mills and Mr. William H. Whyte, Jr., who argue that the bases for personal economic achievement are no longer an aggressive personality and a will to dominate men and the environment, but rather a soft conformity to the ideas of whoever is powerful at the moment and a willingness to immerse oneself in the given mores of the organisation, and to be a loyal subject and a 'front man' for an organisation which supervises one's

every action and guides one's choice in taste, ideas and even
wives. And the 'Organisation Man' in Mr. Whyte's term is,
and is increasingly, the successful man. While it is clearly true
that a modern advertising executive of Madison Avenue could
not succeed if he acted like the Jay Goulds or Rockefellers of
old, the discovery makes some Americans uncomfortable. It
is not just the feeling that Americans may be becoming soft,
it is also that in this, their softest period of history, they have
never been so prosperous.

The conjunction of these contemporary thoughts with the
'image' of the Constitution and political institutions of the
United States, has led to an influential strain of thought which
seems to suggest that the peculiar political constitution of the
U.S. may have had little or nothing to do with its progress as
the accepted success story of Western civilisation. It was the
hard work of Americans who took little interest in politics, the
abundant resources which were provided by nature, not by the
Constitution : the availability of immigrants who were needed
as hired hands not as recipients of the American democratic
religion—these are what has made America what it is. And
to crown the argument one has to hand the assertions of the older
style American ideologues who always insisted that, with the
exceptions of Washington, Jefferson and Lincoln, the really great
Americans were the captains of industry, banking and commerce.

We have now glanced at some of the arguments for and
against the importance of political institutions and attitudes in
the general history of America. There remains another thought ;
however excellent American institutions may have been for
American progress (or however irrelevant), and assuming that
an American standard of living is desired by other peoples, no
other country has ever succeeded in copying the American style
in politics, although many have imported copies of its constitution.

Since the days of George Washington, political institutions
have been adapted to fit current needs, and quasi-political institutions have sprung up to do what formal political institutions can-

not do. All that can be attempted here are some general observa-
tions on the effects of these changes and, to make this theme capable
of treatment in a short essay, attention will be directed to changes
that have taken place in the last two decades. While our primary
concern will be with domestic developments, America's reputation in the world as a whole, the ideology and practice of its
foreign policy, cannot be omitted. I propose therefore to deal
firstly with the assessments which are now being made with
respect to the functioning of formal institutions, the Presidency
and Congress; secondly with the political parties and political
attitudes in the country; and lastly with the question of the
domestic and foreign implications of American foreign policy.

The Presidency was originally conceived of as the office of a
Chief Executive who would have important but limited functions and the holder of which would have been chosen through
the method of an 'Electoral College' of presidential electors
selected by the separate states. The important functions included
the *initiation* (but not the final determination) of foreign policy;
the command of the armed forces of the U.S.; the upholding
of the Constitution and laws of the United States; and the
recommendation of measures to the Congress which the President
considered desirable. He had a veto power over legislation
(not absolute—it could be overridden by a two-thirds vote of
Congress), and, with the consent of the Senate, he nominated
his men to high federal offices. All this meant that an active
President could give a lead in the country, could publicise his
views on policy and, with his right to nominate, and with his
considerable control over 'spoils' appointments in the federal
service, could go some way toward gaining an acceptance for his
political policy. With a Congress in which his own supporters
were in the majority he might achieve much.

It is now clear that a President can do either more or less
than was envisaged by the Founding Fathers: it depends upon
the personality and political skill of the President, the state of
the parties in Congress and the temper of opinion in the country.
Some Presidents have been active, and creative and have
dominated the political scene: others have let Congress run the

country, but it now seems to be generally agreed that the U.S. needs a strong President. He must be strong because he is the only man who can see the total picture of domestic and foreign events; because to an increasing extent national policies are called for at home; and because the American people now expect him to act and think nationally. Moreover according to theorists of an 'active' Presidency like Theodore Roosevelt, the President has a moral right and a moral obligation to behave as a good steward for his country, for he is the only man in America who has behind him a body of national sentiment, congressmen and senators being local men elected not infrequently on local issues. These men are not elected to think or act nationally; they are delegates from local constituents, not representatives in Edmund Burke's sense. All of this argumentation is of course in the field of political rationalisation. The Constitution is silent on these matters.

Under Franklin Roosevelt and Harry Truman the U.S. saw the active Presidency in being and while many accepted it as a necessary concept for our times, influential Republicans argued that it was not a correct conception of the office, and that America would benefit from a spell of inactive Presidencies, milder politics, and relaxation of Federal government meddling with economic life. In fact what the country needed was Dwight D. Eisenhower, an honoured and benevolent military personality whose distaste for politics was, and is, genuine. Under Eisenhower the American people got the ending of the Korean war and much of the relaxation and de-politicising which was promised. Eisenhower's approach has been to let well alone, to continue, even to improve upon the welfare policies of the New Deal, but otherwise to let the country settle down after the hectic days of the New Deal, the World War and the Fair Deal. Eisenhower was fortunate in that the Korean war did end, prosperity did continue, while the Truman Doctrine policies of the previous administration, being quite sufficiently anti-Communist for the Republicans, were continued and developed by Mr. Dulles. President Eisenhower's illnesses removed him for long periods from the personal direction of affairs, but his

Cabinet held together and ruled effectively, so effectively that in November 1956 the voters put Eisenhower in again, despite what must be considered serious medical evidence against the wisdom of his continuing in office. But now in the summer of 1957 it looks as if the whole argument of an inactive President must be opened again. The 'Eisenhower Doctrine' has been announced; the breach with the British and French over Suez occurred; and is there any evidence that the American peoples are more willing to go to war in the Middle East under Eisenhower than they were in the Far East under Truman? If the Eisenhower Doctrine does not commit them to using their military forces in the Middle East, how serious is the doctrine as a device for dissuading potential aggressors? It may turn out that the State Department will achieve its aims in the Middle East by different methods, keeping in reserve the possibility of military action. But doubts will remain as to the real meaning of the Eisenhower Doctrine— doubts which arise from the political, as well as the moral, dilemmas which confront American statesmen who wish to use force against a power whose actions do not affect the immediate physical security of the U.S. On the home front too there are doubts. The 'inactive' President had considerable difficulties with Congress in 1957 over his budget proposals (and is said to have shown little political skill on that occasion), and his Secretary of the Treasury resigned. He cannot, even if he would, run for a third term in view of the 22nd Amendment, so there is no reason now for the Republican party to rally round him as they did in 1956.

The Eisenhower experience seems to illustrate the unreality of believing that in the middle of the twentieth century the United States, which is committed in world politics and world economics on a vast scale, can have at its head a man who as a matter of personal faith believes that most things are best left to work themselves out. It is true that the Eisenhower regime has run concurrently with unprecedented prosperity for the American people. But is prosperity enough? This is the key question, and the answer does not come pat. For the earnest student of international politics in America the answer is a plain negative;

for millions of Americans it might well be an equally emphatic
'Yes.'

In the last twenty years Congress, the legislative arm, the
representative of the people and the watchdog over government
departments, has gradually been reasserting its independence
of the Executive. This process began earlier than we realise.
So impressive and dominant was the personality of Franklin
Roosevelt, who was elected to the Presidency four times, that we
tend to forget that his domination over Congress lasted in fact
for a very short time. From early 1933 to about the end of
1938 his word was obeyed by the congressional leaders of his
party, but from the outbreak of the Second World War in
September 1939 until his death early in 1945 what he achieved,
and it was of momentous importance, was achieved by co-operation with Congress, by skill and guile, and by extensive use of
his powers as Commander-in-Chief. From 1945 until 1952
President Truman struggled manfully and sometimes successfully
to carry on the Roosevelt tradition, and his conception of the
Presidency was as F.D.R.'s. He committed troops to Korea
(note that Eisenhower asked congressional permission for these
powers which were constitutionally his without that permission) :
he vetoed bills; he was in the thick of the political fight domesti-
cally; he won a dramatic victory in 1948 against all the
predictions of the pollsters, and late in his administration's life
he seized the steel industry for the U.S. government to forestall
a national steel strike.

Congress never wholly approves such executive initiative and
during the last twenty years has found its way back to a position
of at least legislative equality with the President. It has dramati-
cally tightened up the immigration laws; it has rewritten in the
Taft-Hartley Act the relations of management and labour; it
has had off-shore oil deposits put under the jurisdiction of the
states rather than the Federal government (because the former
are thought to be more easily importuned by the oil interests
than the latter), and with the permission given to the late
Senator McCarthy it sponsored, or at least acquiesced in, a
vicious denigration of Federal government bureaucrats in general.

It has shown its hostility in a score of ways to the proposition that America needs firm policies designed by Presidents and Cabinets, accepted by legislators and administered by trusted civil servants. On anti-Communism it has not been less vigorous than the administration, but even here it has been scornful of attempts by the administration to work out consistent and reputable policies. McCarthyism at home (with the 'purging' of American libraries abroad) has done incalculable harm to the reputation of America as the world's leading democracy; but for the lack of important evidence to the contrary it must be assumed that Congress does not care about such foreign repercussions so long as, *vis-à-vis* his local constituents, each congressman appears as a convinced nationalist devoted to the task of freeing his beloved country from the insidious influence of foreign ideas and their carriers in the U.S.

The Congress in short has reverted to its customary status of being the place in which local men look at national and international issues from the viewpoint of parochial values and interests. For even on an issue on which there is general unanimity, *e.g.*, the furtherance of a national political and propaganda policy abroad, there is constant congressional obstruction fostered by the desire to cut taxes and control the departments. This political irresponsibility is grounded in an odd constitutional fact, *i.e.*, Congress can both vote huge sums of money for, for instance, the air force and then in the same breath refuse to raise the necessary money by taxes to pay for these forces. Both actions are of legal force, with the result that the money must be provided by putting the finances of the U.S.A. one bit more 'in the red.'

Congress, its organisation and behaviour, and with it the party system that gives rise to this behaviour, has been the subject of scores of articles and books in the post-Roosevelt era. Some reforms of the machinery of Congress were effected by the Legislative Reorganisation Act of 1949. These abolished some indefensible anachronisms of the committee system of Congress, and endeavoured to make the congressman's life a little happier by providing a slightly increased salary, and more expenses, and by giving through the Legislative Reference Service of the Library of Congress better research assistance to the legislators. But these reforms have not radically altered congressional attitudes. Nor has the fact that congressmen are now considerably better educated than they were fifty years ago altered the picture to any great extent. Basically the legislature is still a meeting place of local interests in which great issues are studied from a local angle and where, if national legislation is produced solely by the efforts of congressmen, it is likely to be bad legislation—bad because it merely enacts a common denominator of short-sightedness and prejudice, bad because it contains so many compromises as to be meaningless or bad because it is unworkable. There are exceptions of course. The Taft-Hartley Act was not bad in all these senses—it depends on one's personal views whether it was bad in any sense. It is not an unworkable Act, and that is probably due to the fact that the late Senator Taft was an exceptionally intelligent man, and a very competent politician.

The academics, and some journalists, have taken up the issue of the nature of the American party system and have advised the creation, for each party, of a National Party Council. This would be made up from congressmen, State leaders, members of the party's national committee with the President—or the titular leader of the 'opposition' party—in attendance and would discipline recalcitrant or notorious congressmen and preserve the reputation of the party in the country. The council might also tackle the question, now being gingerly approached for the first time by the national committees of both great parties, of considering future policy and publishing statements and plans about matters of national policy—for at the moment a national party headquarters with a powerful policy and research department is far more a thought than a fact. But these ideas of reform can be written off as almost completely academic. A congressional leader of long standing might be able to see the advantage of such central co-ordination of policy, legislation and candidates, but the average congressman wants to remain undisciplined, able to change sides, and open to suggestion and persuasion by his constituents. He is not worried by grand questions of national party policy. He just wants to get elected and it is up to him to interpret his actions or the words of the nominal leader of his party in any way that he chooses. Nor, it must be added, do the American electors show much interest in a new system of disciplined parties. Most congressmen, they are likely to believe, are not very important men (though the profession of congressman or senator is considered more honourable now than in the past) and if you dislike the representative from your district, you will see that he does not get elected again.

Organisationally the Democratic and Republican parties are not likely to be reformed in the near future. Nor are they likely to shed their customary garments of reputation, personality and past achievements to don new fashions of thought. The Republicans are still the more conservative party overwhelmingly supported by big business and devoted to the American 'free enterprise' principle. The Democrats are the more liberal (in the American sense, which means radical) and receive support from trade unionists, small men, 'immigrant' groups and Catholics. Both parties have had troubled thoughts about the value of these reputations, when the views and interests of voters seem to change more rapidly than the parties' images of themselves. The Republicans have thought of a 'new Republicanism' which accepts the basic values of the welfare state, staunchly protects individual rights against both McCarthyism and the encroachment of 'creeping Socialism' and lauds the old-fashioned virtues of initiative and independence. But the 'new Republicanism' has not taken root, for the old Republicans do not believe in the welfare state, do not disapprove so strongly of McCarthyism and are only really interested in property rights and the menace of 'creeping Socialism.' The Democratic party has hardly gone as far as the Republicans in rethinking and with the effects of its New Deal wearing off (both because Republicans now accept it and because Democrats no longer think it relevant) it has had to rely in the last two elections on the high intelligence, ability and attractive personality of Mr. Adlai Stevenson. But plainly this is not enough, and when faced with the grave problem (for the Democrats) of its attitude to segregation in the land of its most solid support, the South, it utterly failed to satisfy either its Southern or its Northern supporters. It is still, however, the 'underdog' party and even in the prosperous U.S.A. there are underdogs or those who think they are—and the Republicans can be relied upon to make mistakes like any party. With Republicans accepting the idea of old age pensions, unemployment insurance, collective bargaining and an internationalist foreign policy—all achievements of Democratic administrations—and with Democratic voters faced with the reality of an apparently continuing and increasing prosperity, the American parties' need for new ideas is, for those interested in these matters, acute. The average voter may or may not care deeply so long as his social security seems to be assured. There are still real problems about standards of living in the urban slums and in the agrarian south, and the solution of them calls forth familiar remedies in terms of New Deal economics. Nor are the upper-income brackets without their problems, though the solution of these calls for a different approach—if current rumour is any guide there is here a shortage of psychiatrists to deal with complex personal problems arising out of the excess of leisure and gracious living provided by the American economy.

With congressmen liable to vote against their party, voters whose allegiance is uncertain and party leaders eager to appropriate and use the latest 'gimmick' of their opponents in an attempt to swing votes, we come to the position where it is clearly seen that party labels cover a complex of moods, traditions, policies and aspirations, a complex which is rarely the same from one election to another. The New Deal held some voters faithful to the Democrats, but by 1952 many of these had gone over to Eisenhower with their New Deal views unchanged. It is thus the mood of the country, the enthusiasms, the more or less permanent worries of the American elector which may be more important, even in the relatively short run, for an understanding of the politics of America, than the pronouncements of its leaders or the details of legislative change. The three important issues or moods since the end of the New Deal have been, firstly, concern over the increased bureaucratisation of life which the New Deal and the Second World War brought about; secondly, and not unrelated in the public mind to the first, the issue of Communism at home and abroad; and thirdly the split mind of America with respect to its new internationalist foreign policy. The first must be dealt with swiftly by saying that there was a considerable New Deal and war bureaucracy, and that when the New Deal was well bedded in and the war won, the reasons for its continued existence became less apparent. Republicans in 1948 and 1952 said it was 'time for a change,' and in the latter year a change was made from the Democratic Party to General Eisenhower. Very little change was, of course, made in government spending, or in decreasing the number of federal government employees, or even in the general direction of lowering taxation or relaxing federal government activity and supervision. This has been one of the bones of contention between the 'old' Republicans and President Eisenhower.

McCarthyism arose and presented itself as a particularly brutal attack on bureaucrats (who by definition are not to be admired) with the added twist that certain bureaucrats were Communists, and that certain elements in the nation—scientists, products of certain universities, writers and other creative individuals, intellectuals in general—were, because they disliked McCarthy and had no high opinion of congressmen, concealed Communists, perverts, or likely to be disloyal. The whole phenomenon of McCarthyism should be looked at as a product of American social history—as has been so admirably done by Professor Shils in his book *The Torment of Secrecy*—but here we must try to look at it in its political context. Senator McCarthy raised to the highest degree of imaginative fantasy the concerns of the American people about Communist intellectuals in government employment (there were a few), Communist leadership of certain trade unions, Communist writers in Hollywood, Communist aggression overseas, the possession of atomic secrets by scientists and bureaucrats, the control of private American educational and other institutions, the position of the foreign born in the United States, and he gave himself to the American people as the embodiment of true American thinking on all these matters. To doubt McCarthy, when he was at his height was potentially a dangerous (and, as many thought, an unnecessarily quixotic) procedure. He asked for an iron clad conformity, and like the Nazi leaders, he would tell you what this entailed when you had agreed to support his position. Out of this episode almost nobody has emerged with credit. People seemed to rush for cover, betraying their own principles and sometimes their friends as well. With notable exceptions the intellectuals did not fight back with much vigour, the newspapers played it all up—normally on McCarthy's side, and the one man who could have given a lead, President Eisenhower, refused to do so. His reason was that he was so sincerely disgusted by McCarthy that he refused to 'get into the gutter' with him. This was an admirable sentiment for a private individual, but for a President to stand back while the Senator damaged his Foreign Service, threw his civil servants into confusion and slandered his military friends was deplorable. His judgment in this matter was seriously at fault.

Since the end of the Second World War America has launched out as the champion of the free world in international politics. This has been, in the judgment of America's leaders, a necessary change dictated by the emergence of Communist Russia and China as world powers. The change has been made consciously and with full consideration of the consequences by the American people and its leaders, but amongst the mass of those not upon the illuminated peak of national politics—and even amongst some of them there—there is deep but unconstructive questioning, not so much of the wisdom, but of the pains and pleasures of this transformation.

Practical isolationism is dead, but the roots from which it drew nourishment have not been ripped away by the tide of events. As these roots are emotional and historical this is not surprising. From the earliest days of the American republic, the American people have considered themselves as being particularly fortunate in not having to bear the burdens that most other peoples have had in the form of set foreign policies, a large and permanent military establishment and all the paraphernalia of institutionalised and professionalised diplomacy. Open policies, conducted by amateur diplomats, a citizen army recruited for a war, patriotism, improvisation and individual initiative—these were enough. Clearly now they are not sufficient and some part of the agony is due to the feeling that these matters ought still to be controlled by ordinary legislators and vocal citizens, and not professionalised as they are abroad. Along with this sentiment of fortunate status is a keen xenophobia—keen in spite of the melting-pot theory of American society. As the 'foreign' elements (*i.e.*, non-Anglo-Saxon) are as yet incompletely fused in the American mass, nationality, naturalisation, country of origin, and degrees of Americanisation may become sensitive points in discussion when there is a search for the originators of some so-called national disaster. It was part of McCarthy's skill that he opened the weak joints of the not yet completely organic social fabric of the United States, and while he shrewdly avoided the accusation of anti-Semitism and anti-foreign bias, he could yet rely on the vociferous support of all the old-fashioned hyper-nationalistic xenophobes. One result was that groups which felt that they might be isolated and attacked next ran to him for cover instead of banding together to oppose him.

An example of America's unhappy attitude towards its new role was clearly illustrated in the Korean war. The war had to be fought—it was an anti-Communist war—but with what criticism and recrimination! The very forces that represented isolationism then, that took every opportunity to criticise the fact of involvement, both criticised Truman for disciplining General MacArthur whose policy would have extended the war to China, urged further aid to the Formosa Nationalists, *and* praised General Eisenhower when he withdrew American troops having, militarily, done little to damage the Chinese Communists. Isolationism then is still a potent force in America. It began by advocating an attitude that would keep the U.S. out of all foreign wars and has now turned into a criticism of all wars except those in which what the isolationists call American interests are clearly involved. This of course is really no great advance in thinking. During the Second World War the isolationists called for a greater Far Eastern effort and gave lukewarm support to the European theatre of operations. In hard terms of interests and investments this is a difficult attitude to evaluate. America's interest in China—the U.S. not being a great trading nation—is almost purely sentimental and with the defeat and rehabilitation of Japan it is difficult to see why the U.S. is so insistent on maintaining an economic and moral embargo on Communist China—except that it is Communist. In the Middle East too there are contradictions. America cannot desert Israel, but how does it expect to succeed if it encourages the Egyptian government and the other Arab states which are sworn to eradicate the state of Israel? Theodore Roosevelt once advocated the attitude in foreign relations of speaking softly but carrying a big stick. To modern anti-imperialist sentiment this may be a nasty looking policy, but is it, in present terms, more likely to succeed than the Dulles policy of talking loudly and wagging an admonishing finger?

Psychologically, but no longer physically, the United States of America are protected by the barriers of two wide oceans and now behind this protection there are massive air, ground and naval forces. Internally life is abundant, opportunities immense and in these two respects America knows it is the envy of the world. In the good days of the age before world wars and world-wide economic depressions, America was a land of plenty, not merely plentiful resources, but plentiful hands to work, plenty of space in which to operate, plenty of time in which to get things done. This meant in politics and administration compromise, indecision, leisure and laxity, all the time in the world in which to act; the only real enemy was your political opponent who might steal your ideas or your voters. And anyhow, politics was a secondary pursuit; if you had to go into politics at least you should make it run like a business out of which the operator took some profit. Americans know that this age is over, but few can bring themselves to make the adjustments, reforms and re-appraisals of their political life which would draw their political system into the more logical and rational pattern from which most non-Americans think they would benefit.

III
DEMOCRATIC INSTITUTIONS
IN THE
ISLAMIC MIDDLE EAST

III

DEMOCRATIC INSTITUTIONS IN THE ISLAMIC MIDDLE EAST[1]

Bernard Lewis

DEMOCRACY is one of the magic words of our time, with a wide range of different meanings in different parts of the world. In the Middle East too the word has been used in a number of different senses, ranging from parliamentary government to royal condescension. During the last century, however, there has been in the countries of the Middle East a real attempt to apply our kind of democracy, with constitutional government, elected legislatures, and civil rights. Today in most of the Middle East these democratic regimes are in a state of collapse or at least of disrepair. In Egypt, where democratic and parliamentary government has the longest history, the renunciation of the Western form of parliamentary democracy was most formal and final. In Saudi Arabia and in Afghanistan, still at an earlier stage of political evolution, democratic government has not yet been tried. In most other states where the experiment has been made, the democratic regimes have a precarious aspect. Only in Turkey, Israel and Lebanon does Western-style constitutional government seem to be developing with any reasonable prospect of success. Israel and Lebanon are excluded from present consideration as having entirely different backgrounds; Israel because of its predominantly immigrant population, Lebanon because of its peculiar religious and social conditions, which have no parallel anywhere else in the Middle East. The relative success of democracy in Turkey, however, a Middle Eastern and Islamic country which has much in common with the other countries of the Middle East, presents a striking contrast requiring explanation.

---

[1] The following is a revised and expanded version of an article originally published in *Middle Eastern Affairs* (New York), April 1955, pp. 101–8. My thanks are due to the editor for his kind permission to republish it in this way.

Islam was born in a small town republic, among a people just emerging from nomadism. Its earliest political memories are of an elected chief ruling by consent according to custom.[2] These memories are enshrined in the classical formulations of Islamic constitutional theory, and have remained in the background of Islamic political ideas ever since.

But the advent of the Islamic theocracy, by transferring the source of authority from the people to God, removed the consensual and revocable element in that authority. Within a few generations of the death of the Prophet, the Islamic state had been refashioned under the influence of the absolutist traditions of the Hellenistic and old oriental monarchies; the Arab immigrants—as later the Turks—forgot the freer life of their nomadic days as they became part of the ancient city and river-valley civilisation of the Middle East.[3]

For the greater part of its history the political experience of Islam has been limited to autocratic rule. Not until the end of the eighteenth century and the beginning of the nineteenth, when the doctrines of the French Revolution and other movements arising out of it began to percolate to the Middle East, did democratic ideas in the modern sense first reach the Islamic world. The introduction of these ideas seems to have begun with military instruction. The failure of the second Turkish attempt to capture Vienna in 1683, and the humiliating series of defeats that followed, impressed on the rulers of Turkey the weakness of their armed forces as compared with those of Europe. The example of Peter the Great's reforms in Russia encouraged the belief that the adoption of Western weapons, equipment and

---

2 The practice of some orientalists of describing the pre-Islamic tribe as a democracy is severely criticised in a recent work on Islamic political theory by a Lebanese jurist, who argues that the term democracy necessarily denotes organised authority, and cannot be applied to a primitive tribal society which has not reached the stage of constituting a state. See E. Tyan, *Institutions du droit public musulman*, I, *Le Califat*, Paris 1954, pp. 69ff.

3 So that both the Arabs and the Turks are to some extent justified when they blame the loss of their pristine freedom on the influence of the great Middle Eastern Empires. They are, however, at fault in blaming each other for the common fate of nomadic peoples caught up into a settled society. The echoes of another sedentarised people lamenting the happy anarchy of its nomadic past may be heard in the earlier books of the Old Testament.

military techniques would restore the former superiority of Turkish arms. During the late eighteenth and early nineteenth centuries, in Turkey and later in Egypt, an attempt was made to modernise the armed forces and bring them up to the level of contemporary European armies in armament, training and skill. These reforms and training projects were almost all carried out under the guidance of French instructors, usually working in the French language. To receive their instruction and read their manuals, the young Muslim cadets therefore had to learn French—the first time that any important group in Muslim society acquired a reading knowledge of a Western language and sat as disciples at the feet of Western teachers. But these neophytes of Western science soon found that the West had more to offer than mathematics and military science, and that their knowledge of French enabled them to read other things besides their textbooks. Some of these other things were available to them in their own college libraries—that of Istanbul, we know, included a set of the *Encyclopédie,* that of Cairo some writings of Rousseau and Voltaire. We may assume that these and other works were brought to their notice by instructors, many of whom were chosen and appointed by the Government of the French Republic.[4]

The impact of these new political ideas was immediate and striking, and by the early twentieth century not only the westward-looking liberals but even some of the orthodox religious leaders were paying at least lip-service to democracy, and showed their recognition of the power of the democratic idea by claiming it as an Islamic revelation contained in the Koran.[5]

[4] See further, B. Lewis, 'The Impact of the French Revolution on Turkey,' *Journal of World History,* I, 1953, 105–25.

[5] A good example of the line of thought of nineteenth century Turkish liberals will be found in an article on democracy by the Young Ottoman leader Ziya Pasha, '*Ikhtilâfu Ummeti Rahmatun,*' printed in Ebuzziya Tevfik, *Numûne-i Edebiyat-i Osmaniyye,* 3rd edition, Constantinople, 1306 (1st edition 1296/1878), pp. 257ff. The title is a tradition of the Prophet, which may be translated, ' Difference of opinion in my community is an act of divine mercy.' It is commonly cited to justify the co-existence of different schools of Holy Law. The reaction of the pan-Islamists to constitutional ideas after the 1908 revolution is discussed in an important study of Tarik Z. Tunaya, ' Amme hukukumuz bakımından ikinci meşrutiyetin siyasi tefekküründe " Islamcilik " cereyani,' *Istanbul Üniversitesi Hukuk Fakültesi mecmuası,* XIX, 1954.

The Middle Eastern interest in democracy was not purely theoretical. There were also practical attempts to introduce this form of government into Middle Eastern countries. Consultative assemblies of one kind or another appear almost from the beginning of the nineteenth century. In 1808, the reformist Ottoman Grand Vezir Bayrakdar Mustafa Pasha summoned a great imperial assembly in Istanbul, to which he invited high officials, governors, pashas, and notables from all over the Empire, and asked them to approve a far-reaching programme of reforms. In Egypt, Muhammad Ali Pasha convened a consultative council consisting of 156 members, nominated from among officials and notables. It first met in 1829, and thereafter met once a year for a day or more, and discussed such topics as education, agriculture, and even taxes. In 1845, the Turkish Sultan Abdul Mejid went so far as to convene an assembly of provincial notables. Two representatives were to be chosen in each province, 'from among those who are respected and trusted, are people of intelligence and knowledge, who know the requisites of prosperity and the characteristics of the population,'[6] and sent to Istanbul to consult with the High Council. The delegates seem to have been confused by this new and unfamiliar procedure and, not knowing what they were expected to say, preferred to say nothing. Finally, in 1861, the Bey of Tunis proclaimed the first European-style constitution in a Muslim country. It reserved executive power to the Bey, but shared the legislative power between him and a Grand Council of sixty nominated members.

The first tentative experiment with an elected assembly occurred in Egypt, where in 1866 the Khedive Isma'il set up a consultative assembly with a restricted electorate and still more restricted functions. During the period of British occupation the parliamentary machinery was extended and improved, and in 1923 a new democratic constitution, based on the Belgian constitution of 1830–31, came into force.[7] In Turkey the agitation for parliamentary government began in the 'sixties, and in

---

[6] *Ta'rīkh-i Lutfī*, viii, Istanbul, 1328 [= 1910], 15ff.
[7] See J. M. Landau, *Parliaments and Parties in Egypt*, New York, 1954.

December 1876 the first Ottoman constitution was proclaimed. After a general election—the first in Islamic history—a parliament assembled in Istanbul in March 1877. In February 1878 the Sultan dissolved the chamber; the constitution was suspended for some thirty years and did not come into force again until after the revolution of 1908. In Persia the constitutional revolution came in 1906. After the First World War, under the ægis of the mandatory governments, constitutional regimes spread all over the Middle East in what seemed to be a universal triumph of democratic principles.

The process began more than a century and a half ago, when the armies of Napoleon and the ideas of the French Revolution awoke the peoples of the Middle East from their long slumber to a painful awareness of their own weakness and relative backwardness. Time was when the great and civilised Empires of the Middle East had looked down with justified contempt on the barbarous and illiterate peoples of the North and of the West. But Europe grew, matured, and renewed itself, while the Orient, sunk in the torpor of decay, failed to perceive or to understand the changes that had taken place, and continued to cherish—as we of the West still cherish—the dangerous but comfortable illusion of its own boundless and immutable superiority. In the course of the nineteenth century this illusion was at last shattered, at any rate as regards material things, and the peoples of the Orient awoke to a disagreeable reality in which their countries, their resources, their civilisations, even their very souls, were menaced by a West that was rich and powerful beyond belief, and which, in its limitless self-confidence and aggressiveness, seemed to be bringing the whole world within its grasp.

The first and natural reaction of the Oriental to this situation was one of wonderment, admiration, and more especially, of imitation, by which he hoped to win the elusive secret of Western wealth and power. To the eager young Muslim visitor to Europe, in search of that secret, it seemed natural to seek it in those features of European life and government that were most different from his own. One was science and technology.

Another was liberalism which, in the Europe of that time, was the sacred cause of progress and enlightenment, combining the hopes both of the noblest of idealists and the most practical of businessmen and technicians—and what, to the visiting oriental, could be more peculiar, more distinctive of the West than constitutional and parliamentary government? Muslim students returning from their studies in Western universities carried with them new and explosive ideas to their own peoples. The attitude of some of the first constitutionalists is well-expressed in a letter by Sadullah Pasha, describing the Paris Exhibition of 1878: ' In front of the central gate one encounters a statue of freedom; she has a staff in her hand and is seated on a chair. Her appearance and manner convey this meaning to the spectator: " O worthy visitors ! When you look upon this fascinating display of human progress, do not forget that all these perfections are the works of freedom. Under the protection of freedom do peoples and nations attain happiness. Where there is no freedom there can be no security; where there is no security there can be no endeavour; where there is no endeavour there can be no prosperity; where there is no prosperity there can be no happiness ! . . ." '[8]

Nationalism as well as liberalism was in the European air at that time—and both meant the end of the traditional Islamic order. In place of the theocratic Muslim society, in which social grouping is determined by religious affiliation, there came the new and disruptive Western idea of the nation, as a group of people bound together by language and origin, and entitled to political sovereignty. In place of the Sultan—wielding autocratic power as vicegerent of God upon earth and upholder of the Divine Law—came the Western paraphernalia of constitutions and parliaments, parties, programmes and politicians, elections and newspapers and the rest, all very pleasant for the small group of Western educated intellectuals who operated them, but completely meaningless to the great mass of the Muslim population.

All the same, the general attitude towards the West was a

[8] *Numûne-i Edebiyat*, 288.

positive one, and if affection and understanding were sometimes lacking, admiration and respect were usually there. In 1905 the widespread belief in constitutional government as the real source of Western power seemed to receive overwhelming confirmation from the Russo-Japanese war, when the whole of Asia saw with delight how a European great power was defeated in war by an Asian state. There were many who did not fail to note the further significant facts that the European great power that was defeated was the only one that still had purely autocratic government, while the Asian power that had inflicted the defeat was the only one that had adopted constitutional and parliamentary government. In defeated Russia, the Tsar granted a form of constitution and convened the first Duma. It was soon after this that the Persian parliamentary regime was set up, followed after two years by the Revolution of the Young Turks in the Ottoman Empire.

And yet today this great experiment has obviously failed. Though the word 'democracy' still retains enough of its magic to serve as an invocation for many different forms of government, the attempt to introduce and apply the classical West European pattern of freely-elected, multi-party legislative assemblies has been or is being abandoned. The plebiscitary elections and controlled chambers that have replaced them may have precedents and parallels in Europe, but their emergence marks a defeat of the European liberal tradition. One may well ask why this should have happened.

Some causes are obvious. The reforms were precipitate, carried through at far too rapid a pace, without due regard to the conditions in which they were promulgated. They were superimposed from outside, and were irrelevant to events actually occurring in Middle Eastern society at the time. A political system taken over ready-made from another society must fail in many respects to correspond to the different strains and stresses of that to which it is applied. For example, the Belgian constitution works well enough in Belgium, where it is the result of several centuries of Belgian history, and where the Belgian parliament is the apex of a pyramid of responsible elected assemblies which has its base in the Belgian parish and borough councils. But the Belgian constitution translated into Arabic and promulgated in Egypt in 1923 as the Egyptian constitution had far less chance of success. Parliament sat in Cairo, supported and understood by a very limited group of people, but had little connection with life in the villages and even the working-class areas in the towns. The whole political order was unrelated either to the Egyptian past or to the Egyptian present, and was ill-fitted to express Egyptian realities.

In a long period of tranquillity, the peoples of the Middle East might perhaps have succeeded in adapting these borrowed institutions to their own traditions and way of life; but no such period was vouchsafed to them. The pressure of internal and still more of external events left no time or opportunity for experiment and adaptation, and the imported machinery, handled by unskilled operators, broke under the strain or fell into disrepair. Among political leaders the idealism of the first reformers gave way to disappointment, disappointment to frustration, and frustration to a cynicism and opportunism that outraged the moral and religious sense of the Muslim masses and brought the whole concept of democracy into disrepute.

This tide of reaction against Western political institutions met and was swollen by the surging wave of hatred against the West generally. It is our complacent habit in the West to assume that our institutions are in all respects superior to those of Oriental societies, and that any change in those societies in the direction of a greater resemblance to ourselves is necessarily an improvement. In fact it is not always so. Westernisation has brought many great and self-evident benefits to the Middle East —but it has also wrought great injuries, and, human nature being what it is, it is the latter that have received most attention. One of the most important of these is the social and political formlessness of so many oriental countries. In the traditional Islamic society there was an accepted system of social and political functions, loyalties and responsibilities. Admittedly, that system was in decay, as was the whole society—but still it worked and was generally accepted and understood. Most of the damage was done, not by Western rulers and imperialists, but by hasty and energetic native reformers who carried through their Westernising reforms with a ruthlessness and a precipitancy in striking contrast with the cautious conservatism of most Imperial authorities. In the event, they turned out to have destroyed better than they built. While their western innovations often proved superficial and impermanent, their destruction of the old system of social bonds and obligations was final, and left a gap that has not yet been filled. These changes, and the many economic and social upheavals that accompanied them, have unleashed a great wave of hostility against the West and all that came out of it. In different classes and levels of society it finds different forms of expression, in different areas it is connected with different specific grievances, but for most people it takes the form of a generalised resentment against the alien forces that have dislocated their whole way of life.

Nor can the West disclaim all responsibility. There is a case to be made for and against Imperial rule as a stage in political evolution, and the stability of the states that emerged from the former Indian Empire suggests that the Imperial peace was not without its merits. But there is little that can be said in defence of the half-hearted, pussy-footing imperialism encountered by most of the peoples of the Middle East—an imperialism of interference without responsibility, which would neither create nor permit stable and orderly government.

These difficulties, augmented by the well-known economic upheavals and political grievances of the Middle East, suffice in themselves to explain the failure of a form of government which, as in the nineteenth century, though with the reverse effect, is associated in the public mind with its western countries of origin. But it may be useful to carry our inquiry beyond present circumstances and to try to see how far the nature of Islamic political and social traditions will favour or discourage the eventual emergence of democratic government.

Despite the traces of nomadic freedom surviving in classical Islamic legal theory, the political traditions and experience of Islam are almost entirely autocratic. The citizen owed, as a religious duty, absolute and unquestioning obedience to the sovereign, and had no rights other than that of living the good Muslim life. The sovereign was bound to observe the Holy Law and to make possible the good Muslim life, but apart from that he could do as he pleased.[9] Islamic theory has never recognised any source of authority other than either God or power. The pious regime—that of the Caliph—derives its authority from God. The only alternative source of authority is power— material and effective power, which may however receive a sort of *post facto* divine approval if the holder of power recognises and maintains the Holy Law. In either case the sole source of authority within the state was the sovereign, who could grant revocable and delegated authority to various persons to carry out his will. All authority was thus personal. Islamic law does not recognise corporate persons, and Islamic history does not show any elected bodies or corporate authorities. Thus there was no state but only a ruler, no court but only a judge, no city but only a conglomeration of families, quarters and guilds.[10]

On the other hand there are certain elements in Islam which provide a possible basis for democratic development. One of these is the traditional tolerance of Islam in both race and religion, which is perhaps one of the cardinal virtues of Islamic society. That does not mean to say that Islam has been entirely free from race prejudice or that it has ever conceded equality to followers of other religions in the Islamic state. Its record however on the whole in these matters is infinitely better than that of any society to the west of it. Even in the greater test of toleration of heresy the record of Islam is extremely good. A striking example is the simultaneous existence of four schools of

9 For some recent views on the Islamic theory of sovereignty, see H. A. R. Gibb and Harold Bowen, *Islamic Society and the West,* Vol. I, Part I, Oxford, 1950, Chapter 2, ' Caliphate and Sultanate,' pp. 26–38; E. Tyan, *op. cit.*; Bernard Lewis, ' The Concept of an Islamic Republic,' *World of Islam,* 1955, pp. 1–9; *idem,* ' Communism and Islam,' *International Affairs,* January 1954, pp. 1–12; G. E. von Grunebaum, *Islam, Essays in the Nature and Growth of a Cultural Tradition,* London, 1955, pp. 127–40; A. K. S. Lambton, ' Quis custodiet custodes? Some Reflections on the Persian Theory of Government,' *Studia Islamica,* 1956, V, pp. 125–48; VI, pp. 125–46.
10 Cf. J. H. Kramers, ' L'Islam et la Democratie,' in *Orientalia Neerlandica,* Leiden, 1948.

canonical jurisprudence differing from one another on a number of points but nevertheless recognising one another as orthodox. This method of agreement on fundamentals with a limited measure of disagreement on matters of detail seems to provide a promising basis for the development of that capacity for co-operation in opposition which is an essential feature of parliamentary government.

Some features of Islamic society which are often adduced by romantics and apologists as 'fundamentally democratic' would probably be better described as equalitarian. There is however a great deal of social democracy in Islam, both in theory and in practice. In the Islamic world from medieval to modern times there has always been a considerable degree of social fluidity, and humble social origin has never been a barrier preventing a man of talent from reaching the highest offices of the State. The point was vividly made by Adolphus Slade, one of the most perceptive of all Western visitors to the Middle East. In 1831, when Mahmud II had already begun to destroy the old order and prepare the way for the great reforms of the Tanzimat, he wrote : 'It is curious to observe the similarity of advantages which are enjoyed by nations in opposite spheres of knowledge, and separated by perfectly distinct manners and religion. Hitherto the Osmanley has enjoyed by custom some of the dearest privileges of freemen, for which Christian nations have so long struggled. He paid nothing to the government beyond a moderate land-tax, although liable, it is true, to extortions, which might be classed with assessed taxes. He paid no tithes, the *vacouf* sufficing for the maintenance of the ministers of Islamism. He travelled where he pleased without passports; no custom-house officer intruded his eyes and dirty fingers among his baggage; no police watched his motions, or listened for his words. His house was sacred. His sons were never taken from his side to be soldiers, unless war called them. His views of ambition were not restricted by the barriers of birth and wealth : from the lowest origin he might aspire without presumption to the rank of pasha; if he could read, to that of grand vizir; and this consciousness, instilled and supported by numberless precedents, ennobled his mind, and enabled him to enter on the duties of high office without embarrassment. Is not this the advantage so prized by free nations? Did not the exclusion of the people from posts of honour tend to the French revolution?'[11]

This kind of freedom and democracy, well-rooted in local tradition, was not increased but reduced by the Westernisation of government. The old and well-tried checks on the Sultan's despotism were one by one abolished; the old intermediate powers of the army, the bureaucracy, the provincial notables and the religious hierarchy were abrogated or enfeebled, leaving the reinforced sovereign power with nothing but the paper shackles of its own edicts to restrain it. This too was seen with uncanny prescience by Slade: 'When a nation, comparatively barbarous, copies the finished experience of a highly civilised State, without going through the intermediate stages of advancement, the few are strengthened against the many, the powerful armed against the weak. The sovereign, who before found his power (despotic in name) circumscribed, because with all the will, he had not the real art of oppressing, by the aid of science finds himself a giant—his mace exchanged for a sword. In scanning over the riches of civilisation, spread out before him for acceptance, he contemptuously rejects those calculated to benefit his people, and chooses the modern scientific governing machine, result of ages of experiments, with its patent screws for extracting blood and treasure—conscription and taxation. He hires foreign engineers to work it, and waits the promised result—absolute power. His subjects, who before had a thousand modes of avoiding his tyranny, have not now a loophole to escape by: the operations of the uncorroding engine meet them at every turn, and, to increase their despair, its movement accelerates with use, and winds closer their chains. A people thus taken by surprise, and thrown off their guard, will be centuries before they acquire sufficient knowledge—every beam of which is carefully hid from them by the clouds of despotism—

---

[11] Capt. Adolphus Slade, R.N., F.R.A.S., *Record of Travels in Turkey, Greece, etc.* [1st ed. 1833], 2nd ed., London, 1854, pp. 144–5.

to compare their situation with that of their neighbours—
(who, although ruled by the same means, have advantages to
counterbalance its weight)—to assert human rights, and to dare
to say "we are men."'[12]

The traditional Islamic kind of social democracy has never
found any political expression, and has been greatly impaired
by the changes of the last century. It remains however deeply
rooted in Muslim sentiment and tradition, and the outrages
offered to it are among the most potent causes of the present
discontents of Islam. It may yet serve as a basis on which some
form of political democracy could be built, though it could
equally well be exploited in another direction.

More directly relevant to political life is the Islamic doctrine
of the rule of law. The Islamic sovereign though an autocrat,
is no true despot. He is not above the law but is subject to the
law no less than the humblest of his slaves. It is true that as a
restriction on the autocratic powers of the sovereign this is rather
theoretical. For one thing the law itself concedes him almost
absolute powers; for another the law provides no machinery
for its own enforcement against the will of the sovereign. Nevertheless it is broadly true that Islamic sovereigns, with very few
exceptions, have maintained the basic principles of the Islamic
law at least as far as was required by the public opinion of
their time, and respect for law has remained one of the deepest
instincts of Islamic society.

The relative success of democracy in Turkey, where the
parliamentary system is standing up well under severe strains,
requires separate explanation. It is difficult at this early stage to
distinguish symptoms from causes, but some features may be
noted. One of the most striking is the greater realism and
responsibility of the Turks, who feel able to adopt a practical
approach to problems and thus to make decisions related to facts
and abide by them. Unlike their neighbours, the Turks have
always been masters in their own house, and indeed in other
people's houses too. Their political thinking has in consequence
not been bedevilled by the problem of foreign rule and the

[12] *ibid.*, 143.

struggle to end it. The process of westernisation and reform has
gone very much further in Turkey than in any of the other
countries. Turkey's foreign policy has shown much greater
awareness of the Russian danger, of which they have long and
direct experience. Finally—and perhaps this is the most important of all—the economic and social changes which have taken
place since the republic was established have transformed the
social structure of Turkey and given her a social order that
provides a much sounder basis for democratic development. It
has often been asserted by critics that many of the economic
development projects carried through by Kemal Atatürk and
his successors were economically wasteful and inefficient. This
may be so, and it may well be that in purely economic terms
they were not worth while. Nevertheless, in the light of subsequent events, it must be agreed that these reforms, however
much open to criticism on economic grounds, have justified themselves in terms of their social consequences. These may be seen
in the emergence of a new middle class of business-men, mana-
gers, technicians, and the like, self-confident and self-assertive,
increasingly critical of the older ruling groups of civil servants,
landowners, and military men, and increasingly assertive of their
own rights. It is this group, more than any other, that has
made possible the working of parliamentary government in
Turkey, and offers the best assurance for its preservation; it is
at least arguable that until such groups appear in the other
countries of the Middle East there is little prospect of an orderly
development of free institutions.

Meanwhile, there is a more urgent choice that the peoples
of the Middle East are being asked to make, between the Western
and Soviet versions of democracy. Which are they likely to
choose?

Despite the hatreds and resentments of recent years, the West
still retains tremendous prestige; just as the individual shows
or claims membership of the dominant social class by wearing
European clothes and shoes, so the well-dressed State with pre-
tentions to modernity must sport a constitution and an assembly
chosen by some form of election. Today America offers the

Middle East a new model of western democracy, buttressed by the immense wealth, power and prestige of the United States, and free from the colonial memories that still attach to London and Paris. At first sight the prospects of American-style democracy in the Middle East would seem to be good. In fact, however, there has been little disposition to follow American practice, and such constitutional and governmental procedures as have been borrowed have come from the southern and not the northern half of the Western hemisphere. Nor are Middle Easterners willing to accept America as something generically different from Europe, and untainted with the European past. For America is still part of that Romance and Germanic, Protestant and Catholic Western Christendom that is the historic West—the millennial adversary of the Islamic Empires, and the source of the devastating impact that has convulsed the Islamic world in modern times. Of this West America is now the conscious leader, and she can no more renounce her association with it than with her language and her culture, her religion and her institutions.

America, then, is also a target—is becoming the main target —of the anti-Western feeling that is so potent a force in Middle Eastern politics. Russia, on the other hand, is not part of the West. On the contrary, she is in a state of conflict with the West, and is for this reason, as were the Nazis in their day, able to muster much sympathy and support. Whatever her behaviour towards the Turkish and Persian speaking Muslims of the U.S.S.R., she is not compromised in Arab eyes by any previous record of domination or interference in Arab countries. The solutions she offers to the great problems of economics and politics have a simplicity and finality that are at once attractive and familiar. In the Middle East, as in many other parts of the world, it is authoritarian and not democratic government that is best known and best understood, and the capricious dictatorship of Moscow has not the strange and repellent aspect that it offers to the Western observer. The West should surely do what it can to encourage the growth of free institutions, 'but at the same time, we would do well to recall that for a great part of the human race, parliamentary democracy remains something remote, alien and incomprehensible, an object sometimes of wonderment, even envy, more often alas of mistrust and hatred, which we must concede is not entirely unjustified when we recall the examples of democracy by which alone they can judge it. If the peoples of Islam are forced to make a straight choice, to abandon their own traditions in favour of either Communism or parliamentarianism, then we are at a great disadvantage.' [13]

It is, however, inaccurate as well as inexpedient to represent the world's dilemma as a straight choice between Communism and parliamentary democracy. Islam is an independent civilisation, different from both the Western and Communist worlds, and the possibility still remains that the Muslim peoples, recovering at last from the trauma of westernisation, may evolve some form of government within their own tradition.

One thing however must be clear from the start. We must not judge the peoples of other countries entirely by what *we* feel to be appropriate. The machinery which works well in the West may not work in other countries. Except perhaps in Turkey, our kind of democracy appears to have failed in the Muslim Middle East. But why must we assume that our kind is the only kind? Perhaps in the course of time the peoples of the Middle East will succeed in giving the word democracy a meaning more suited to their own experience, more closely related to their own traditions, more expressive of their own aspirations. As we have seen, there are antecedents of a kind in Islam for such a development. An elected head of State and the rule of law are familiar. It is true that the first has been purely theoretical, and has not been applied since the days of the first Caliphs in any Islamic State of high material civilisation —but if the doctors of the law of medieval times were able to reduce the electorate to one, there is no reason why their modern heirs should not extend it to a wider suffrage. The Muslim rule of law is theocratic rather than democratic, deriving its authority from the immutable revelation of God and not from the changing will of the people—but the principle is admitted, and the

[13] Bernard Lewis, *Communism and Islam*, 2.

range of interpretation is vast. Equality and fraternity within the faith-group are accepted and old-established—perhaps it may be possible to extend them beyond it and, adding a redefined liberty, to make a new kind of democracy.

Only 'the question is' as Alice remarked, 'whether you *can* make words mean so many different things.'

IV
DEMOCRATIC INSTITUTIONS
IN AFRICA

IV

DEMOCRATIC INSTITUTIONS IN AFRICA

ROLAND OLIVER

IN thinking about democratic institutions in Africa and their prospects for the future, there are two things that need to be remembered from the start : first that the period of real impact by the West upon Africa has been very short indeed; and, secondly, that despite this fact the impact of the West upon African life has been revolutionary and overwhelming to a far greater extent than it has been, for example, anywhere in Asia. One must remember that from the middle of the fifteenth century until the middle of the nineteenth, for the first four centuries of modern times, Africa meant only two things to the nations of Europe. First and foremost, it was a gigantic obstacle on the routes to the East. Secondly, it was a source of slave labour for the mines and plantations of the New World. Consequently Europeans sailed round Africa. They established tiny fortified settlements at various points around the African coastline. But they did not penetrate. Their activities affected African life deep into the continent, but only in an indirect, negative, destructive way. It was only in the nineteenth century, and for most of Africa in the very late nineteenth century, between 1880 and 1900 in fact, that Europe entered Africa in sufficient force to start to do anything constructive. And even then, the deliberate planting of democratic institutions came a long way down the list of priorities. After all, however fantastic it may seem when one looks back on it today, I suppose that even to the most liberal-minded Europeans of the 1880s and 1890s it would have seemed quite certain that the new European empires in Africa would last for several hundred years. And even right down to about ten years ago, I suspect that the imaginary time-scales which most thinking Europeans had in mind for African self-government, or the full participation of Africans in government, was something which was calculated in terms of two or three generations and not in terms of one of two decades. Let the reader search his own memory on this subject. What were his ideas in 1939? And what were they in 1945? And what are they today? The comparison of any truthful answers to these questions will be deeply disquieting, because it will show how little the actual situation facing us in Africa today is one which has been consciously planned and prepared for. It will show that European administrations in Africa have been working, no doubt in all good faith, but in illusory expectations and to false time-tables. It will show beyond a shadow of doubt that power will have to be transferred to governmental structures that are at best but half complete, and to hands and minds that are inexperienced and little trained. It will show, therefore, that the thing upon which we have to build our hopes in regard to democratic institutions in Africa, is not so much what has been deliberately planned and placed there by European governments, but rather the ideas which have caught on almost insensibly through contact with European people, and above all through the spread of western education. We have to trust in the spirit and intention of African nationalism to carry forward a process which has barely been begun.

And here, fortunately, it does seem that the overwhelming nature of the all too brief European impact upon Africa does give some grounds for optimism. For in Africa, at least in Africa south of the Sahara, it is not merely that vast areas have been conquered or otherwise occupied by European nations. It is not merely that the government has fallen temporarily into alien hands. It is not merely that the economy has been revolutionised. It is not merely that some western ideas have been sown in schools and universities. All these things have happened in Africa, but they have happened in large parts of Asia too. And, despite all these things, there has remained in Asia a solid substratum of cultural resistance to the impact of the West. The majority of educated people in all the Asian countries have felt that there was enough solid ground under their feet for them to be able to pick and choose from the offerings of the West. By and large they have taken the technology of the West, but they have left the religion. They have taken some of the political ideas, but they have left others. Whereas in Africa south of the Sahara, I venture to say that the disturbance caused by the impact of the West has gone much deeper, even though the impact of the West has been felt for a much shorter time. Of course there are parts of Africa, especially in the south and east, where Europeans have made permanent settlements, where they have not merely conquered, administered, taught and traded, but where they have actually taken possession of much of the land and minerals in private ownership, and where they have used both political and economic means to build themselves into a ruling class. That has naturally involved a much greater disturbance of African life than any Asian people has had to suffer. But there is another side to the story, which is just as true of those parts of Africa where Europeans have not settled as of those parts where they have settled, and which is seen, for example, in the fact that nowhere in Africa have the pagan, tribal religions been able to stand up against the impact of the West. Islam, yes. Northern Africa, Islamic Africa, that has stood up to the strain. But Africa south of the Sahara, pagan Africa, has gone under far more completely than any Asian culture. Of course paganism still exists all over Africa, but it is strictly fair to say that it is in the remoter places and in the older generations. The new Africa, which has come through the European impact successfully, to the point at which it is now actively challenging European political dominance, is an Africa which has, to a very large extent indeed, identified itself with western values, including even western religious values. The African nationalist leader of today is a nationalist precisely because he has absorbed western political ideas; and if he lives anywhere to the south of Northern Nigeria or the northern Sudan, the chances are a hundred to one that he has absorbed them in a Christian school, and ten to one that he himself has, at some time and in some loose sense of the word, accepted the Christian faith. Now this is a picture very different indeed from the picture anywhere in Asia. It is certainly true that in Africa the new educated class is still pitifully small, smaller even than it is in most Asian countries. But, in the realm of ideas, it has less need than any Asian educated class to find an intellectual compromise with the past. And so the dangers to democratic institutions in Africa are not primarily ideological

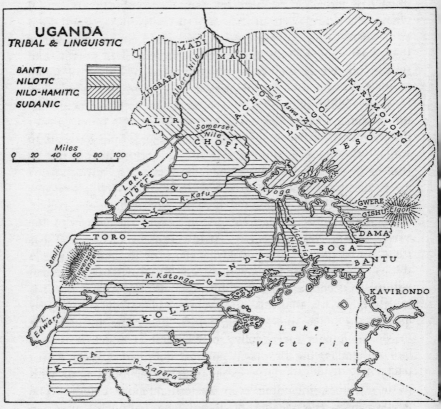

dangers. They are dangers on the one hand of political frustration leading to calculated revolution and destruction, and on the other hand of local loyalties leading to fragmentation and chaos.

With these two preliminary generalisations in mind, let us turn to the situation as it was eighty to a hundred years ago, when the European nations took over, and let us try to see what seeds of democracy were already present in the indigenous political systems. It is not an easy line of inquiry, because one is faced at the outset by the immense range of African political institutions, a range so stupendous that it almost defies classification. Let any one who is curious examine for a start the admirable volume entitled *African Political Systems,* edited by Professor M. Fortes and Professor E. E. Evans-Pritchard, and he will at once see that there is hardly a generalisation that can be made which holds true for all, or even for half of them. Nor does it help to carve the continent into regions, and to take it region by region. There is no overall difference between East African political systems and West African political systems. The whole range of differences is fully represented in both. They are all jumbled up. The most authoritarian, centralised states lie geographically next door to the most loosely organised, tribal groups which have no central organisation at all. And the new territorial frontiers created by the European nations run quite quixotically across major tribal and linguistic boundaries, making confusion worse confounded.

Perhaps the best way to paint an adequate picture of the situation in a small space is to take one modern African territory, for example the Uganda Protectorate, and to examine briefly the varieties of African political systems which are included within its boundaries. It is quite a small country : about the same size as England, without Wales or Scotland. From the modern capital at Kampala you can reach almost any part of it in one day's hard motoring. It is inhabited by about five and a half million people. It is, so one might suppose, a nice, compact, convenient, administrative unit. But now just look at some of the complications. To start with, those five and a half million people speak, not four different languages, but four different groups of languages, that is to say groups of languages built up on quite different principles, as different from each other as English and Welsh. South of a line from Mount Elgon to Lake Albert the languages spoken—and there are about ten in all—are of the Bantu family. In the North-East, Teso and Karamojong are Nilo-Hamitic languages. In the North Centre, Lango and

Acholi belong to the Nilotic family. In the North-West, Lugbara, Madi and Kakwa are of the Sudanic group. All these groups of languages are mutually quite unintelligible, and yet the peoples who speak them have somehow to grow together, and very soon, into a single modern state.

So much for the languages. The political systems are still more varied. At one end of the scale there is the kingdom of Buganda, as African political units go, a large one, with a population of a million and a half. Now Buganda has, and did have ninety years ago when the first Europeans passed through, a most unusually efficient and highly centralised political system. At the head of the state there was the king or *kabaka*, who was an absolute monarch, perhaps not quite in the same sense as our own Plantagenet kings, but at least in the same sense as the early Tudors. The Kabaka of Buganda a hundred years ago was perhaps rather like Henry VIII in the power that he enjoyed. What was most remarkable about the system in African terms was that the *kabaka* ruled through an elaborate hierarchy of chiefs—there were seven grades of them, ranging from the county magnates right down, as it were, to the village magistrates —and these chiefs were not hereditary feudal barons, but administrators appointed during the king's pleasure, who could be moved about from one job to another, and promoted or demoted at will. The most important of them were expected to have town-houses at the capital as well as country houses in their own districts. They had to keep the roads in repair between the country and the capital. They had to administer justice in their own districts, and also to maintain a constant supply of labour and produce for the support of the king and his court. Besides this administrative organisation there was a military organisation, and even a naval organisation of war-canoes upon the lake. There was also a most elaborate social organisation whereby the principal members of all the main families or clans were chosen for ceremonial functions about the court, and bound by matrimony into the royal family. And finally all these institutions, administrative, military, social and ceremonial, were represented in the *kabaka's* Privy Council or *Lukiko*. It was not of course an elected body. It existed not to legislate but to give advice. It was not perhaps a very democratic institution : indeed we know little enough in detail of how it worked. But no doubt the various interests represented exercised in practice a considerable check on the absolute power of the monarch. Certainly, taken all in all, there was in Buganda a set of political institutions by no means worthless as the basis of a modern system of local government at, say, the County Council level.

But let us look now at the other end of the scale, keeping for the moment within the Bantu-speaking, southern half of the Protectorate. In the south-western corner you have the mountainous district of Kigezi. On the eastern frontier of the territory you have the westward-sloping valleys of Mount Elgon. In each of these districts there are large Bantu tribes, of about 400,000 people each, called the Bakiga and the Bagishu. But these, a hundred years ago, were tribes only in the sense that they each spoke a common language, and in the sense that they were made up of a number of clans whose girls and young men normally intermarried with each other rather than outside the language group. There were no central political institutions at all. There were no hereditary rulers, even of the myriad little valley units in which these peoples lived. They were mountain peoples, who were relatively secure from outside attack. They did not need to combine for defence, or for any other purpose, in the simple life of subsistence agriculture which they lived in pre-European times. And so they remained almost unorganised until they were overtaken by civilisation in the shape of the Protectorate Government, which began in the early years of the present century to drive roads up their mountain valleys, and to levy taxes, and to build schools and hospitals, and to do various other things among them which required a central organisation and, above all, some executive power. The Bakiga and the Bagishu were democratic all right. The trouble was that they were democratic to the point of anarchy. Certainly they were too democratic to survive in the conditions of the modern world. And so, in these districts, the problem of building up modern institutions of local government was quite different from that in Buganda. It was a matter of concentrating power, not of dispersing it.

Lastly, for an even more extreme example of the problem, look at the north-eastern corner of the territory—at Karamoja— a large district, 200 miles from north to south, of dry, grassy plains. Here the determining factor of the environment is not mountains, but water. The population of some 150,000 was not even static. They were cattle-keepers, moving from pasture to pasture, stopping only to take a quick crop of manioc from beside the river bank in the rainy season. When I was last there, in 1950, the men were stark naked, the women were in skins. I think I am right in saying that no administrator had ever learned their language, and that in order to communicate with them, even for example for the purpose of holding a murder trial, it was necessary to use, not one but two interpreters, one to translate from Karamojong into Teso, and one to translate from Teso into Luganda or English. It was all very picturesque, I remember. The man who looked after the Government rest-house arrived in the morning, planting his spear in the flower bed in the front garden, and hanging up his bow and arrows beside the kitchen sink. But as to democratic institutions, either now or in the foreseeble future, it is very hard even to guess. And yet the Karamojong are by no means unique in mid-twentieth century Africa. Indeed, there is almost no territory one can think of between the Sahara and the Cape which does not contain some groups of people who fall into the same category.

Most of the peoples in Uganda, and for that matter in most other African territories too, come, as regards their own indigenous political systems, somewhere between the two extremes, represented by the Baganda on one hand and by the Karamojong on the other. There is no such thing as a typical situation, but if you wanted an example of something between the two extremes, you would find it in Uganda among the Acholi or the Basoga, where the institution of hereditary chieftainship existed, but not on the basis of one chief per tribe, but of many chiefs, perhaps twenty or thirty, each ruling sections of a tribe, some ruling 10,000 people, others ruling a few hundred, with no

central authority above them. In other words, looked at from
the point of view of modern democratic institutions, there was
in these districts something which could serve as the basis for a
series of Rural District Councils, but nothing which could serve
as the basis of a County Council. And there are other districts
again—such as the Teso and Lango districts of Uganda—where
the institution of chieftainship was unknown, but where there was
an indigenous basis for, say, Parish Councils, though not for
anything more centralised.

Summing up, therefore, the problem of creating democratic
institutions of local government, one might say that it consisted in
the fact that in almost every African territory there was this
almost infinite variety of indigenous political institutions all
jumbled up together, a centralised system next to a decentralised
one, a sedentary, agricultural group next to a pastoral, nomadic
one, a tribe with hereditary chiefs next to a tribe without chiefs,
and so on. And the next stage of the inquiry, therefore, is to ask
what has happened during the past sixty to eighty years of European rule to transform these local institutions, and to iron out the
differences between them. And here I think one can distinguish
two successive stages which followed each other in most parts
of colonial Africa, and the recognition of which throws a good
deal of light on the problems of today. Remember, the question
at this stage concerns the institutions of local government in the
districts, and not yet the new institutions of central government
which were being set up by the European powers at their colonial
capitals. It concerns the District Commissioner sent out by the
colonial government to govern one tribal area, and how that man
tended to treat the tribal institutions which he encountered.
Because I think one would find that, whether he was an English-
man, a Frenchman or a Belgian, whether he represented a
settler government as in Southern Rhodesia or a Protectorate
type of government as in Nigeria, the pattern of that man's
activities were remarkably similar from one end of the continent
to the other.

It is important to remember that at the start the District
Commissioner was often, quite literally, just one man, with only

a small detachment of African soldiers or armed police behind
him. His primary job was to maintain law and order, to super-
vise the administration of justice and to collect the taxes. And
there could be anything up to half a million people in his care.
Naturally a man in this position was eager to use any institution
that he found ready to hand. Only, of course, he was not
primarily interested in democracy. He was interested in getting
things done. He was interested in building up a strong executive. He wanted to find people who could give orders, who could
turn out a labour force to build a road, who could collect taxes,
who could deal with petty crime. And so he seized on the
institution of chieftainship wherever it was to be found, and
where it was not to be found he usually invented it. Moreover, right through the early years of his rule, the District Commissioner was mainly intent on building up the executive and
judicial functions of chieftainship at the expense of the ceremonial and deliberative functions. He was turning the rain-
maker into a local government official. He was turning the
recipient of honorific tribute into a salaried collector of taxes.
Very often this meant deposing one individual and substituting
another. If the hereditary principle was strong, he would
probably depose the father and substitute a son, perhaps a son
who was still a minor, perhaps a son who had been educated
at one of the new mission schools. If the hereditary principle
was less highly valued, the District Commissioner would very
likely introduce a nominee of his own into the chiefly office, one
of his own trusted clerks or interpreters, or perhaps a competent
police sergeant, who had no connection at all with the ruling
family. Broadly, therefore, it would be true to say that the first
thirty years of the European District Commissioner's activities
in Africa brought about a great ironing-out and transformation
of African political systems, which was of vital significance for
the future of democratic institutions of local government, and
also of some significance for the long term welding of district
and district into the wider framework of modern states. In this
stage of the process the District Commissioner himself became the
local autocrat or 'divine king,' and the former divine kings, if

any, became his local government officials. It may seem para-
doxical that in many places the first step towards western
democratic institutions lay in the strengthening of individual
authority; but, if so, one must remember that to us in Europe
democracy has meant the dispersing of power which was
previously in the hands of a few, whereas among many African
peoples it has meant concentrating power which was previously so
widely dispersed as to be almost anarchic.

But however much the District Commissioner may have
acted as a transformer and unifier, there was one concession
which he nearly always made to the past, which was to become
of greater and greater importance as time went on, and which
is seen today as almost the most crucial question of all for the
future of democratic institutions in Africa. That concession
was that, willy-nilly, the District Commissioner nearly always
continued to govern African peoples in their own language units.
International frontiers sometimes cut clean across the territories
of certain tribes, but within a single colonial territory district
boundaries very seldom did so. The effect of this has been very
profound, because it meant that, however much the political
institution of a tribe may have been transformed and standardised, the modern local government system which has emerged,
has nevertheless emerged upon a tribal and linguistic basis. The
new local government unit has been supported by tribal sentiment, and in a very large number of cases one could actually
put it the other way round, and say that the tribal sentiment
has been strengthened by the introduction of the new local
government institutions. And this is an aspect of the matter
which has become more and more important in modern times,
as the District Commissioner has moved out of his initial position
as the 'divine king,' as the supreme, autocratic ruler of his
District, into his contemporary position of 'Town Clerk.' As
the Chairman of the 'District Team,' comprising the Resident
Magistrate, the District Education Officer, the District Agricultural Officer, and all the other specialists of modern local government, he has become the convener of every sort and kind of
committee from the Township Councils to the local agricultural

producers' co-operative societies. More and more local people
have been drawn into the machinery of local government. The
initial emphasis on a powerful executive has given way to local
government by council and committee, with the result that even
the tribal groups which were previously the most loosely organised have developed a strong feeling of local, tribal patriotism.
A few African tribes have always had this feeling—the Baganda,
for example, in Uganda, the Yoruba in Nigeria, the Ashanti in
Ghana. But the remarkable development of the last twenty
years or so has been the emergence of this feeling in other groups
which did not have it before—among the Ibo of Eastern Nigeria,
for example; among the Ewe of Togoland and Ghana; in
Uganda, among the Acholi, the Lango, the Teso, the Basoga.

The significance of this strengthening of local, tribal feeling
as a result of the development of local government institutions
becomes apparent immediately one turns to a consideration of
the contribution of the central, colonial governments, which
form the growing-points for the new nation-states of Africa.
Because the one essential point to grasp in this matter is that it
has been the central machinery of the colonial government—the
Governor, the Secretariat, the Legislative Council, the High
Court, and so on—that has been the brand new, and completely
foreign importation into the tropical African world. The District
Commissioner has been, technically, a part of this new government. But he has only been its local representative. He has
been identified primarily with the tribe and the local community;
and whatever the changes he has made, the local government
he has built up has been regarded by the people as *their* government, staffed for the most part by *their* people. Whereas the
central government, at Salisbury, or Lusaka, or Zomba, or
Dar-es-Salaam, or Entebbe, or Nairobi, or Leopoldville, or Lagos,
or Accra, has been regarded right up until today as the government of the foreigner, staffed by the foreigner, and built up on
foreign ideas. And not the least foreign of these foreign ideas
has been the strange notion of erecting one government over
many tribal groups which have traditionally regarded each other
as foreigners, if not as enemies.

At this point I should mention an important and stimulating recent book, *Must we lose Africa?* by Colin Legum, the African Correspondent of the *Observer*. The first section of the book is a straightforward account of the crisis in Uganda following the deportation of the Kabaka in 1953, and this section has an interest of its own. But I would draw attention especially to the second part of the book, in which he argues that in most of Africa the tribal spirit is going to prove too strong for the success of the present policies, and that the only way to avoid disaster to the democratic institutions we are building, is to abandone our traditional methods, in favour of *federal* systems of central government, which will allow the tribal units of local government to have the greatest possible share of power. I think this is a view which needs to be taken seriously. One has only to look at the present situation in Ghana and in Nigeria to see the force of it. At the same time I am not myself convinced that Legum is right. I look at this problem as an historian, and throughout this argument I have laid great stress on the historical development. And the point that seems clear to me, in view of the history, is that, whereas the development of local government institutions is something that has been impinging directly on African life for a very long time, central government has been until quite recently something very remote and artificial to the majority of the African peoples. And furthermore, whereas no colonial government in West, East, Central, or even South Africa has had many inhibitions about developing local government institutions for Africans in African areas, almost every colonial government has been slow and confused in associating the African populations with the central government institutions. Even in West Africa and the Sudan, where there were no European settlers to worry about, central government posts were regarded for many years longer than was necessary as a European preserve. In Uganda, where again settlers have been a negligible factor in government, it is only now, in the late 1950s, when Africans are already in a majority in the central legislature, that African civil servants are being recruited to the administrative class of the central civil service. This is a situation that has its dangers. But on the whole I do not feel as despondent as Legum and many other people do about the long-term persistence of the tribal spirit. It is certainly one of the gravest dangers to the development of strong, democratic nation-states in Africa that, during the early years of their self-government, comparatively mature local government institutions will be tempted to try to break away from comparatively immature central institutions. It may happen in Ghana. It may happen in Nigeria. But at least let us remember that, despite one major explosion in 1955, it has *not* yet happened in the Sudan, despite the existence of a situation of almost unparalleled tension between the South and the North.

This brings me at last to the question of the multi-racial societies. I have already hinted that in the mono-racial societies of West Africa, the Sudan and Uganda, the local government institutions are not unsound, but the danger is that the central government institutions tend to get taken over and Africanised terribly suddenly, before there are enough educated and experienced people to operate them. And so this handful of educated people, having won their independence, are left struggling to hold together a vast, illiterate majority, whose interests and loyalties are still local and tribal, rather than national. The danger, therefore, is the danger of fission. In the multi-racial societies, the development of *local* government institutions has once again been fairly impressive. But the trouble in this case has usually been, at least under the British systems, that the *central* government institutions have passed, at a fairly early stage, more or less into the hands of the immigrant European communities, who have proceeded to entrench themselves, and to obstruct the participation of the indigenous inhabitants, as these have become politically conscious on a national, as opposed to a merely local, scale. How successful they have been in entrenching themselves has depended almost entirely upon their numbers. In the Union of South Africa their numbers have reached nearly three millions in a total population of some thirteen millions, and it is just nonsense to suppose that any metropolitan power in Europe could have stopped them from doing what they have done. They were bound to take power into their own hands at a very early stage. They had the numbers and the resources to run all the machinery of government without any co-operation from the indigenous peoples, and with the disparity in education and skills, it was inevitable that, having once acquired power, they should take all measures to keep it in their own hands. The consequences for democratic institutions are obvious, and I need not dwell upon them. I think that it is useless to expect any major changes in the South African regime, until things have changed a lot more farther north. When the white South Africans find themselves occupying just the tip of a continent, the rest of which has succeeded in eliminating race as a factor in the political scene, then they will rethink their position, but not before.

Moving north to Central Africa, the Belgian Congo and East Africa, the numerical proportions are very different. In the Federation of Rhodesia and Nyasaland there are some two hundred thousand whites to some six million blacks, a proportion of one in thirty. In the Belgian Congo and East Africa there are in each case something like sixty thousand whites to twenty million blacks, a proportion of roughly one in three hundred. In the Belgian Congo nobody, black or white, has as yet any democratic rights in respect of the central legislature, which is controlled closely from Belgium. The Belgians argue that it is wrong to give political power to Europeans in Africa until you are prepared to give them to Africans also. They also maintain that it is wrong to give political rights to a small élite of educated Africans, who would use them to exploit the uneducated majority. It is therefore necessary to wait for the masses to catch up. This is at least a consistent policy as far as it goes, and so far it has proved remarkably successful in practice. But it leaves little scope for comment about democratic institutions at a central, territorial level. One can only await with interest for the *dénouement*.

In British Central and East Africa on the other hand, the policy has been to introduce central, legislative institutions at an early stage, but to introduce them on an aristocratic principle. This can take one of two forms. On the one hand you can have what is called a 'common roll,' in which the aristocratic principle takes the form of a high educational and property qualification. This is the system in force in Southern Rhodesia, where, incidentally, the property qualification is at present so high as to exclude all but a few hundred Africans. Or, on the other hand, you can have a system of communal voting, whereby each race is represented by a fixed number of seats in the central legislature, and you have a certain number of official, civil service, members to hold the ring. The aristocratic principle in this case lies in the deliberate allocation of seats in such a way that the minority races are represented out of all proportion to their numbers. Theoretically, the common roll is the better of the two systems, because it emphasises qualifications rather than race, and because it is self-adjusting. As soon as a man acquires the qualifications, he acquires the vote. Whereas in the other system, if you want to change the allocation of seats between the different races, you are faced with a constitutional change, and you have got to persuade or bully the entrenched minorities to agree. And that, of course, is something that you can only do if you are, not merely theoretically but actually, in control. In theory the United Kingdom government is still in control everywhere north of Southern Rhodesia. But, actually, it is very doubtful if it is, since the Federation, in a position to influence the electoral situation in either Northern Rhodesia or Nyasaland. So that effectively leaves Uganda, Tanganyika and Kenya. In Uganda, I think, there is already no doubt which way things are going. It will be surprising if, within ten years, there is not an effectively self-governing African state in Uganda. And there seems to be every prospect that progress towards it will be orderly. There should be time for the central legislature and the central civil service to become very largely Africanised and to gain the allegiance of the component peoples before the final transfer of power takes place. In Tanganyika it may well be the same. For, though Tanganyika has settlers, both European and Asiatic, they are much more mixed in nationality than in Kenya, and politically much less firmly entrenched. In Kenya, however, the Europeans will, on their present showing, dispute fiercely every successive advance of the Africans in the central legislature, and the danger is that if constitutional advance is blocked, the temptation to use violence will recur, especially where, as in Kenya, the visible opposition is so small that there appears to be a sporting chance of success.

The multi-racial territories, therefore, like the predominantly African territories, have the problem of attracting to their central legislatures the allegiance of the masses of the people. They can solve it only by greatly extending the range of political and economic opportunity; and in so far as they fail to do so, they will face the danger of violent fission. Only, unlike the predominantly African territories, the tendency to fission is less likely to be motivated by a desire to return to the autonomy of the component tribal groups. It will, more probably, take the form of attempts by peripheral groups to transfer their allegiance to neighbouring states, where the opportunities are seen to be greater. Already, in East Africa, Uganda is beginning to exercise a sentimental attraction among the neighbouring peoples in Western Kenya, North-West Tanganyika and Ruanda-Urundi. East Africa as a whole exercises a corresponding attraction for the politically frustrated groups in Nyasaland and Northern Rhodesia. It is becoming yearly less possible to insulate African territories, with their long land frontiers, from the influences at work among their neighbours. For the future of democratic institutions an element of competition between neighbouring states could well be an advantage, providing that it is recognised in time by those who exercise power. If unrecognised, it could bring nascent democratic institutions to an untimely and violent end.

It is obvious that in Africa the student of political institutions can at present do little more than examine the foundations of democracy that have been laid during the past half century by the invading powers of the West. It is too early to measure with any certainty the nature of the African response. Probably no movement of imperial expansion in the world's long history has succeeded in retaining control until its work of education was completed. Only in Africa it must seem in retrospect that the opportunity of the West has been greater, and its moment of power shorter, than it has been in other parts of the world. Owing to the poor and fragmented development of most of Africa at the time of the western penetration, the West has been able, not only to bequeath a pattern of political institutions, but also to sow in Africa seeds of western religious and moral values to which Asia and the Middle East have been largely impervious. The ecclesiastical institutions planted by the West in Africa are a factor which must tend to buttress the political institutions. But according to all the indications western control over both the political and the ecclesiastical institutions will have to be abandoned long before they are safely consolidated under educated indigenous leadership working under the sanction of articulate public opinion. Effective power will have to be transferred to minorities, whether white or black. It is too much to expect of human nature that these minorities will always act as the disinterested trustees of the masses. Democracy in Africa, no less than in Europe, will remain a privilege that has to be fought for : but if the western powers depart from Africa having brought most of the continent to a stage of political development equivalent to that of England on the eve of the Great Reform Bill, they will nevertheless have achieved something of importance in the world's history.

V

THE IMPACT OF
WESTERN DEMOCRACY
ON ASIA

V

THE IMPACT OF
WESTERN DEMOCRACY ON ASIA

Hugh Tinker

ANY suggestion that democracy is a gift bestowed by the West upon less politically mature nations would be rejected by almost every Asian of today. The pattern of Asian democracy, they would contend, has been worked out by Asia's thinkers and leaders themselves, and the right to 'government of the people, by the people, for the people' has been earned and won by Asians themselves through long and arduous struggle against the dominance of the West. And yet, looking back to the traditional societies of Asia, it is difficult to discern any approach towards the values of democracy.

If democracy has a central theme it is, surely, the concept of the responsibility of the governors to the sovereign people. The people must be able to exercise a choice, to decide who is to govern them : and, even more vital, they must have the opportunity of revising or reversing their choice, of changing the government. And 'the people,' for practical purposes, means the electorate, who in making their decision at the polls are equal and individual : one man, one vote. One man : a political unit, not to be identified with a tribe, community, religion, trade, calling, or any other badge or caste. One vote : no gradation according to social or economic status, no weightage for intellect, years, or experience, but common political equality. The practical working of democracy depends upon acceptance of the principle of counting votes to determine the opinions of the people by separating the 'ayes' and 'nos,' the 'ins' and 'outs.' This implies acceptance of the verdict of the majority, and the acquiescence of the dissenting minority in the advancement of men and measures by the majority—which the minority hopes and expects to replace one day with its own.

Almost every one of these ideas is contrary to the custom and belief of Asia, if one can generalise about the manifold cultures of this vast area.[1] To whom, in the traditional Asian view, is the government responsible? Most political systems of Asia seem to answer, to God or Heaven. Even today, the Constitution of the Islamic republic of Pakistan begins 'In the name of Allah, the Beneficent, the Merciful : Whereas Sovereignty over the entire universe belongs to God Almighty alone, . . . the authority to be exercised by the people of Pakistan . . . is a sacred trust . . . ,' and this is no mere form of words. The Muslim ruler of old owed a duty to God to govern according to the precepts of the Koran and the *Shariat*. A good Muslim ruler was one who submitted to the will of God. The Emperors of China and Vietnam governed their peoples under the Mandate of Heaven. This did not represent an active supervision from above, but when a dynasty was successfully established after a period of anarchy, the 'mandate' was considered to have passed to the dynasty. When a ruler failed to uphold good government, the lapse of the mandate was foreshadowed in men's minds by natural disasters : floods, famines and earthquakes. Wherever in Asia some sort of contractual relationship between governor and governed is discernible, it is almost always one in which the ruler commands the allegiance of his people because, in a semi-divine form, he personifies and secures the prosperity of the realm.[2]

Government in Asia was absolute and despotic. In Burma and Siam, under certain circumstances, the royal council of ministers played a part in the choice of a successor to the throne, but almost everywhere a ruler nominated his own successor. This could only be challenged by a pretender who was prepared to stake all on a bid by force. Once upon his throne, the ruler was supreme, appointing and dismissing his ministers, rewarding or punishing, as he thought fit. The only limitation upon his power

1 By ' Asia ' we are considering mainly South and East Asia, from Pakistan to Japan, an area with a population of some 1,300,000,000 ; Russian Asia and the Middle East are excluded.
2 For example, the King of Burma annually took part in a ceremonial ploughing of the royal lands near the capital. This ' Royal Ploughing ' ensured the success of the year's paddy crop.

lay in the traditional rules of custom and religion and in hereditary rights.

The key to the relation between society and the individual
was status : hereditary position, determined not by individual
ability nor even by the accumulation of wealth, but by birth and
relationship. The most complex example is, of course, provided
by caste in India. The countries of South East Asia are sometimes thought of as relatively 'democratic' under their old
kings, being almost entirely caste-free societies. But even in
these lands, hierarchy and status formed the framework of society.
For instance, in Siam the *sakdi-na* concept, a mathematical
grading of men in the social scale, regulated exactly the place
of all men from Prince down to district official; or in Burma,
a man was liable to State service as a musketeer, a cavalryman,
or a war-boatman not by reason of personal fitness but according
to hereditary prescription.[3] Only in China was it possible to step
out of one's place in society : within narrow limits. The highly
developed civil service structure made it occasionally possible for
a youth in humble circumstances who was also a scholar to rise,
by competitive examination, to the highest grades in the man-
darinate. But even this system was tempered by the entrenched
advantages of the official families which enabled them to favour
their own family candidates in many cases.

Granted that the ruler was absolute, answerable, if at all,
to Heaven, and that society was hierarchical, with the individual's
place in the social order predetermined by birth; still, some
would argue, in the village council—a thriving institution in
many Asian countries—there existed the germ of democracy. In
India, the village council, the *panchayat*, formed the focus of
village life. Its decisions were accepted by all members of the
community and its deliberations were conducted at length and
in open forum, reflecting and interpreting public opinion.[4]
Similarly in Java the village or *desa* had its communal organisa-

---

[3] In Burma it was theoretically possible for any educated man to attain
high office, but in practice these offices were generally held by members
of certain ' official ' families.

[4] See the writer's *Foundations of Local Self-Government in India, Pakistan
and Burma,* 1954.

7

tion and its system of village co-operation. Indeed, whether one looks at the Empire of China with its highly-developed administrative system, or at the tiny, rustic hill states of the Indo-Chinese peninsula, one sees village self-government almost everywhere.

But certain aspects of Asian village self-government differentiate it from Western concepts of democracy. First, it exists to interpret established law and custom, to regulate the activities of persons in an almost static society governed by tradition. Second, it is based upon acceptance of hierarchy and inherited privilege or abasement. The village chief or headman will invariably be drawn from one family of hereditary leaders, and the village elders will generally come from certain specific families or callings. The 'underprivileged' will have no voice in village affairs; and yet—this leads to the third difference from Western democracy—the decisions of the village council, reflecting as they do established gradations of the social order, do nevertheless reflect the feeling of the village as a whole. Even in caste-bound India, the humble sweeper or unclean leatherworker are accorded their due, meagre though this may be. The village council has never arrived at conclusions by counting votes : invariably, it has worked towards the 'general will' of the whole village community. Such a method is, of necessity, slow, subtle, and involved : quite a simple problem may not be solved until the council has debated for a full week or month, night after night. But at the end, by an almost mystical transmutation of ideas, not the majority, but the whole community has arrived at a corporate decision.

If we return to the basic suppositions of Western democracy, they are seen to conflict at almost every point with those of the Asian 'village republics.' It must be acknowledged that the reception of democracy, the adoption of a diametrically opposed system of values has come about through the intervention of the West in Asia. The Western colonial Powers (with the exception of the United States) manifestly did not conquer their Asian territories in order to transplant self-government on a Western model in their colonies. Indeed, they entertained the gravest reservations about the suitability of Western democratic institutions for Asia, right up to the twentieth century. Nevertheless, in practice, the successful absorption of democracy has been accomplished only in the former colonies.[5] A glance at Persia, Siam, or Afghanistan will serve to illustrate the point. Moreover, it might be arguable that those countries which underwent the most thorough experience of colonial rule (India and Ceylon) are precisely those where democracy today is most successfully accepted and assimilated.

Foreign conquest appears to set off a cycle of reactions from the subject people which has followed a regular pattern, not only in Asia but in Africa and elsewhere. At first, when the advance-guard of the West appeared, its strength was often underestimated, so that a lodgement was gained in the guise of a trading company or a church mission within the Asian or African country with the acquiescence, or even, occasionally, the approval of the indigenous Sovereign. Then, as the West established its hold, imposed its government, its laws and economic practices upon the Asian society, a violent endeavour would be made to eject the now unwanted intruder. The indigenous Power would make the only response it could : a challenge at arms.[6] Being no match for the West in terms of firepower, discipline, or logistics, it was defeated : usually, decisively. There might follow a period of blank acquiescence in defeat, when the Asian felt that he was powerless to oppose Western superiority; but sooner or later, elements in the population would be brought into association with the Western administration or Western economic enterprises, and would begin to absorb Western techniques. From these 'associates' came a demand for Western education and a share in the activities introduced by the West : the administration, law, journalism, business. At first, the process of learning and association was undertaken in a genuine admiration for Western thought; undertaken in a conviction that the Asian

---

[5] Japan may appear to be a partial exception to this dictum : but the American occupation, 1945–52, formed the most intensive 'colonial' experience applied anywhere in Asia.

[6] Hindu India had a more effective weapon, the all-embracing caste system which had, in large measure, passively resisted the pressure of the Muslim invaders. But there are solid grounds for arguing that the Mutiny of 1857 was the militant reaction of the old India.

could only make his way in the new, wider world if he assimilated himself to the Western model; in effect, if he became in his thought-processes and behaviour a Westerner. Having absorbed the new learning, the new Asian went on to demand Western political institutions. The pioneers of political reform looked to the Colonial Power to pass on these institutions as a father passes his birthright to his son, but even in the rare instances where there was a sympathetic response to such demands there was considerable disagreement concerning how and when political enfranchisement should follow. And so the Westernised national leaders to an increasing extent regarded the Colonial Power not as a 'parent' but as a harsh guardian, a jailer. National movements went back more and more to their own history and their own cultures for inspiration in the struggle against Colonialism. In some instances the renascence involved a synthesis of old and new, domestic and foreign ideas that represented a new level of political philosophy: such was the Gandhian achievement in India. Elsewhere the return to historical attitudes has blurred the concept of a national political ideology introduced by the Westernised reformers: this is part of the present problem of Indonesia. Traditional culture can be degraded and perverted in the revolt against Colonialism and the West, as with Mau Mau in Kenya.

The essential point is that in this latter phase of the absorption of democratic ideas the teaching of the West has been turned against the West. Today in Asia, as a consequence, Western dominance has been withdrawn, and new, independent countries proclaim their adherence to democracy. In some countries, notably in Ceylon and India, the new democracies are founded upon freedom movements of almost a century's standing; in others, such as Laos, Cambodia, or even Malaya, it is difficult even yet to detect any coherent political consciousness at all: yet these countries too have opted for democracy as their chosen form of government. The extent to which democracy has become a native growth, has shed its foreign or textbook flavour is an obvious yardstick of development. Yet even in the most politically mature Asian countries comprehension of the meaning of democracy is limited : strongly developed among an educated élite, diffused in ever cruder terms among the circles of the less educated and less sophisticated, and apprehended only as a dimly understood if powerful phenomenon by the masses, the rural peasantry and the city coolies. It may clarify the picture to classify, albeit somewhat artificially, the different layers of political experience that have emerged in South Asia and, to a lesser extent in the Far East.

The standard bearers of political development have been the Westernised upper middle classes, those brought most intimately into contact with European life and thought, either by their professional vocations or by their social standing. The first impact of Liberal ideas upon Asia came about almost entirely through this medium : reference to India and Ceylon in the late nineteenth century, Burma in the 1920s, or Malaya in the 1940s will show the importance of this class as the 'seed bed' of political growth. Far the most important group were the lawyers whose experience of the English legal system led naturally towards a demand for concomitant political institutions. Almost every leader of importance in Southern Asia has undergone legal training; many have practised at the Bar, and some have sat on the Bench.[7] Among names far too numerous to mention at length, the law has produced in India, Pheroz Shah Mehta, Motilal Nehru, C. R. Das, Sardar Patel and, mightiest of all, Gandhi; in Pakistan, Jinnah and Suhrawaddy; in Ceylon, Goonetilleke, Kotelawala and Dudley Senanyake; in Malaya, Tungku Abdul Rahman; in Singapore, David Marshall. The world of journalism—or more strictly, those English-language newspapers which have modelled themselves on *The Times* or *Telegraph*—has also been influential, as witness Surendranath Banerjea, editor of the *Bengalee*. The university world has produced distinguished leaders : in the early days of political development, the ladder provided by scholarships, teaching posts and professorial chairs was almost the only means whereby a poor boy could make a political career, as was shown by

---

[7] The continuing preponderance of lawyers in Indian politics, right down to the present, is emphasised by W. H. Morris-Jones, *Parliament in India*, 1957, pp. 114–28.

Dadabhai Naoroji and G. K. Gokhale in India, and Sir D. B. Jayatilaka in Ceylon. Medical men, retired senior officials, and rentiers or absentee landlords also played their part in forming a political 'climate of opinion.' The Westernised upper middle class has been concentrated, to a large extent, in the great metropolitan centres which have arisen as the result of Western commercial and industrial connections : Calcutta, Bombay, Colombo, Singapore, and other maritime cities, where an Asian middle class associated with Europeans as partners or rivals in business and the professions.[8] Here political life began, first at a municipal and then at a national level as a natural element in public affairs.

These cosmopolitan, urban Asian families were the pioneers of European education and, from the middle of the nineteenth century, they sent their sons to England to study and read for the Bar. This section of Asian society, minute though it is, has supplied the top-rank political leadership of Southern Asia right down to the present day : Jawarhalal Nehru, Prime Minister of India, educated at Harrow School and Trinity College, Cambridge ; M. A. Jinnah, *Qaid-I-Azam* of Pakistan, who practised in the highest courts in England alongside the leading English Counsel : Tungku Abdul Rahman, Chief Minister of Malaya, scion of a ruling family, a member of St. Catharine's College, Cambridge ; S. W. R. D. Bandaranaike, Prime Minister of Ceylon, of Christchurch, Oxford : these are the men who have guided their countries upon the threshold of independence. All came from wealthy, middle class households, all have been called to the English Bar ; they are men who, in Nehru's words, 'think in English' ; men who have achieved a deep understanding of Western political theory and practice ; who, in themselves, stand forth as interpreters of the democratic tradition, who combine a Western outlook with an Eastern voice.

But such men are few ; the rank and file of political organisation and agitation is provided by the lower middle classes. This definition includes all who are literate in English, to whatever

[8] A delicate picture of the Anglicised Calcutta upper middle class is painted by N. C. Chaudhuri, *Autobiography of an Unknown Indian*, 1951, pp. 396-7.

extent; all who own any parcel of land or a dwelling, however modest; all who operate any kind of shop or business. These classes are, of course, numerous in the cities, but their prevailing background can be described as small-town or rural; their archetype is the village schoolmaster or the trader in the market-town.

What contribution have these elements made to political evolution? Many from the lower middle classes will have attended a local university, especially in India where the graduate who is a poorly paid clerk or even unemployed is an all too familiar figure. But education on the Western pattern will have made only a limited impact. University study is often a nightmare, the cramming of undigested facts temporarily into the student's mind for the sole purpose of securing a pass in the B.A., the essential gimmick for any sort of advancement in Asia. Traditional patterns of belief about religion and society will exercise a dwindling influence over thought and behaviour, while new ideas absorbed from a Marxist handbook or as a result of student agitation will deposit a sediment of angry emotionalism. Of all the social groups, the lower middle class is probably the most restive in Asia. Clerical workers in particular receive a miserably inadequate return for their labours: an assistant in a merchandising business, a hack reporter, or an office scribe will be paid less than a bus driver or a skilled artisan. And so, the lower middle classes with their resentment at their depressed status and their incoherent awareness of the new forces in politics are in ferment. The more astute find an outlet on their national political bandwagons, become district organisers, M.P.s, perhaps, eventually, Ministers. A superficial view suggests that these successful politicians then find a place in the upper class milieu and cease to express the feelings of their under-privileged brethren. This is not the case with the Communist leaders,[9] and the appeal of Communism to the lower middle class, economically unstable and politically volatile, forms a factor of importance in the future of Asian democracy.

[9] Compare the Communist campaign in the Indian parliament in 1954 to oppose all proposals for the introduction of salaries for M.P.s.

The lower middle class has already produced a few leaders of the front rank to stand beside the upper class statesmen. Mr. Don Senanyake, the first Prime Minister of Ceylon was the manager of a small plumbago mine; U Nu, Prime Minister of Burma, is the son of a small-town trader; Lim Yew Hock, Chief Minister of Singapore, is a former trade union organiser. The 1956 General Election in Ceylon (which is certainly the most advanced society, in the political field, in Asia) was interpreted by some competent observers as marking the arrival of the lower middle class as the key force in Ceylon politics, despite the continuation of the Westernised minority in the highest offices. By the 1960s a similar trend may be discernible in India.

The lower middle classes, even in the widest terms, constitute no more than 10 per cent of the population : the great mass of the people are simple tillers of the soil. About eight out of every nine inhabitants of Asia live in the country-side,[10] and among the urban proletariat a high proportion came themselves from the country. As we have noticed, the background to rural life everywhere throughout Asia (except for the nomads and the hunters) is the village community, and its pattern is the pattern of Asian life. An intimate, custom-regulated society, it has no tradition of participating in outside affairs : traditionally, the arrival of representatives of the government, even if they represented a reasonably humanitarian regime, was greeted with suspicion and apathy. Government was absolute, an autocrat to be obeyed, and no concern of the village community. The village had one great preoccupation : to feed itself, and this (except in a few favoured lands in South East Asia) was and is a struggle. Recent (1951) calculations put the annual income of the peasant in different countries at the following figures : Japan, £50 ; Ceylon, £42 ; Siam, £29 ; Pakistan, £23 ; India, £18 ; Burma, £13. It is true that these figures should be doubled, or in some cases trebled, to provide a reasonable basis of comparison with current European money values : but when all adjustments have been made the picture is still one of extreme poverty. And so, the

[10] In India in 1949 there were less than two-and-a-half million factory workers out of a total population of 357 million.

politician who aspires to obtain the support of the village must make his appeal in a special way. He has first to overcome the invisible barrier which the village has thrown up against all who govern. He must take care not to offend the religious susceptibilities and other traditions and loyalties of the village folk. Above all, he and his party to appeal successfully to peasants battling for survival, must present their programme in basic terms. Peasant ownership of land, improved irrigation, reduced taxation : these are subjects the peasant understands are important, but he is unlikely to be moved, for instance, by controversy over foreign policy.

The Asian peasant, like most peasants, is no fool : if he assumes an ox-like manner towards strangers, that is part of his defence mechanism. He is capable of judging men pretty shrewdly. He is practical and not averse to innovation in matters affecting his job as a cultivator, providing these do not clash with his religious beliefs : for example, Japanese methods of rice culture have been widely and rapidly adopted in India and Ceylon by the ordinary peasant : but suggest that he improves his cattle by destroying unfit cows and he will return a blank refusal. In matters of the mind he still obeys the precepts that have guided his ancestors for hundreds of years. Any generalisations about rural Asia made today are liable to be outdated tomorrow : but for the present, the peasant has grasped that his vote is an instrument of power whereby he can play some part in the destiny of his country : the actual processes of politics and government are still remote, beyond his grasp.

In some measure the village is educating itself. Radio, government information services, village reading rooms, adult literacy classes, have all arrived to bring the world to the villager's doorstep. Young men from the village enlist in the armed forces and are thereby introduced to a new range of technical knowledge and new modes of behaviour in regard to hygiene, dress, spending, etc. Other youngsters take jobs in transport or on the new development schemes, or go off to work in the big cities. All this means that almost every family has a foot in the wider world, with inevitable effects upon accepted village standards.

Because of the extension of adult franchise throughout the greater part of South and East Asia, every peasant is involved—if only once every five years—in the national political debate; for this reason, to an ever-increasing extent, he will be the object of attention from his governors and those who seek to govern him. There is a striking difference between the generation of peasantry in India (as an example) twenty-five years ago, who never really emerged from their ancient world of custom and tradition, and the generation of today, on the brink of the modern world. But the difference that will follow between this generation and those who are now but babes will be infinitely greater.

Meanwhile, it remains true that the Asian masses are politically mute and await the emergence of leaders from their own patient ranks. Under the conditions of today the peasants still cannot create their own leadership. Among the Communists this is equally true. Mao Tse-tung, who comes from a prosperous family of farmer-merchants, was educated in a teachers' training college; Chou En-lai is the son of a Mandarin family, and almost all the other Communist leaders are intellectuals of bourgeois origin.[11]

Perhaps we may now proceed, finally, to analyse the process whereby democratic ideas have entered into the life of Asia. We have seen that the idea germinated with an intellectual Asian élite, and was then carried through ever widening levels of society and, in a fashion, across the boundaries of different Asian countries, as from India to Burma and Malaya. Over a century ago, Macaulay propounded a theory of education for India : he suggested that Western liberal principles would filter down through society, from a minority of university graduates, through the high schools and the middle classes to the village schools and the millions. It is commonly supposed that this 'filtration' policy completely failed in its purpose, that Western education has remained ever since Macaulay's day the prerogative of the middle class. Yet in the political sphere Macaulay's 'filtration' theory has been substantiated : middle class Asians absorbed Western

[11] Than Tun, the principal Burmese Communist leader, is a partial exception; he came from a poor family and worked as a village schoolmaster before entering politics.

political principles and proceeded to interpret them to the mass of the peoples of Asia. Political ideas have been disseminated by a process of simplification : from the complex intellectualism of a few, to a rudimentary creed for the multitude. During this process, Western political ideas have become Asian, in emotional content if not in intellectual outline. To reiterate what was earlier called 'the cycle of reactions' : during the nineteenth century Asian reformers enthusiastically adopted the teaching of the West as their own, but at a later stage in the national movements this teaching was permeated with indigenous feeling and was turned against the West in its guise of Imperialism. By the middle of the twentieth century, something like a synthesis had been achieved in the most advanced countries, India and Ceylon, at the level where political decisions are shaped and decided : parliament, the press, the universities, the civil service. At the level of the village, or even of the local government authority, a conflict continues between East and West, and in less developed Asian countries the conflict continues at the national level.

Let us now examine the Western models which Asia looked towards in the nineteenth century. It is not merely national pride or prejudice which would seek to place the British contribution first : whatever suspicions may still linger regarding British Imperialism, British ideas and institutions have been adopted and acclimatised throughout wide areas of Southern Asia and are now accepted, their foreign origins overlaid by native usage.[12] The first and perhaps foremost English 'loan' was the transplantation of the Rule of Law to Asian soil. This introduced the concept of law as absolute, common in its application to all people ; applied by a judiciary that was apart from the influence or pressure of the executive. It was not so much the actual application of English law in India, Burma or Malaya that was important : English laws did become a part of their usage, but Hindu, Muslim and Buddhist law remained in force in many

[12] When the writer arrived at the University of Rangoon as visiting Professor of History, he was first asked to teach English Constitutional History. He was told ' We are independent, but we have adopted the English parliamentary system so your constitutional history is now our history.'

fields, for instance in all matters of inheritance : but the important innovation was the absorption of the spirit of the English
legal system. The concept of equality before the law, of the
equality of Brahmin and untouchable, of landlord and peasant,
of European and Asian; the concept of the independence of
the judiciary, of the subordination of even an autocratic government, such as the British Government of India, to the Rule of
Law, the refusal to recognise any species of *droit administratif,*
so that the courts may not be overruled by administrative fiat :
acceptance of such principles into the climate of educated
opinion formed an essential prelude to the acceptance of the idea
of individual liberty and democracy.[13]

A second British innovation was the creation of a free press
in Asia. Freedom of the press was established early in the nineteenth century in India (against the advice of many British
officials, it must be said) by British professional men and missionaries in Calcutta and Bombay, and a free press was created in
all the British territories in Asia. The right to criticise the government (though it may become destructive and negative when no
opportunity is offered actually to remedy affairs) is another
essential prelude to political experience. Independent criticism
of authority was unknown under Asian rulers, as it was in
medieval Europe. Another political institution built up during
the 'colonial' period was a non-political, professional civil
service, an administrative élite, of which the Indian Civil Service
was the first and the greatest. Under democracy, the people
may voice their desires through the politicians, but unless an
efficient civil service exists to give effective shape to these desires,
democracy has no meaning : this is particularly true in a new
country which is attempting to launch vast new schemes of
development. The former British dominions in Asia are now
better served by their civil services than, for example, such
advanced democracies as Australia or the United States. A corps
of administrators with a high tradition of service, hard work,

[13] It is not suggested that these principles were always upheld in practice
by the British in Asia : but the very exceptions, such as the notorious
'Rowlatt Act,' emphasise the importance which was attached to the
ideal.

responsibility and incorruptibility has provided India, Pakistan and Ceylon with backbone and brains during the first critical decade of independence.[14]

As the demand for political institutions developed, it was met by the setting up of Legislative Councils whose non-official members were selected as the representatives of some community. This principle of representative deliberation was a significant departure from the Asian tradition of public assembly (so far as one existed) which was the gathering together of all members of the community, as in the Indian *darbar*. Last of all came the setting up of parliaments, with Ministers responsible to these parliaments, and jointly associated in Cabinets under a Prime Minister. Viewing the Asian scene in 1957, the only states to have successfully established the parliamentary, cabinet system have been those formerly under British rule or influence : the collapse of parliamentary government in Indonesia, compared with its endurance in Burma, despite every kind of obstacle, provides a striking example. Time alone will determine how much weight can be attached to this differentiation.

If Britain's legacy has been mainly practical, the creation of institutions, that of America has been largely inspirational, the diffusion of a moral idea. As the first people to proclaim that colonial rule was an evil, to shake off the yoke of the metropolitan country, to establish a moral claim to freedom and the Rights of Man, the United States loomed largely in the mythology of Asian colonial peoples. The folk-heroes of the American Revolution, such as Paul Revere, were taken into the pantheon of Asian middle class youth. Probably the high-point of American prestige was attained with President Wilson's enunciation of the doctrine of national self-determination : this phrase echoed throughout Eastern Europe and across the world, giving impetus to the freedom movements in India, Indonesia and elsewhere. Thereafter, the emotional role of the United States as the torch-bearer of liberty declined. Today, Americans have to face the

---

[14] It is noticeable that those Indian politicians and British radicals who were loud in their criticism of the ' sun-dried bureaucrats ' in pre-independence days are today unstinted in their praise of the service rendered today by those same ' bureaucrats.'

accusation that they have been false to their own anti-colonial tradition : today, they are singled out as perpetuating 'colonialism' and 'imperialism' : unworthy charges, but moral fervour is an unstable, uncertain quantity to deal in. America's contribution in the field of actual institutions has been more restricted. The practice of endowing the President with power as Chief Executive has been imitated only in America's own colony, the Philippines, and (to an extent as yet undetermined) by America's protégé, South Vietnam. Elsewhere, presidents are intended to act as purely ceremonial heads of State. The full implementation of democratic ideals in the shape of universal adult franchise was first accepted as a practical proposition in the United States ; but Asians today are more likely to remember the exclusion of the American negro from his rights, in this connection, than to acknowledge the American origin of the practice. The election of officials, as practised in America : the election of postmaster, judge, sheriff, and all, has not been followed in Asia outside the Philippines.

Other sources of inspiration to middle class nineteenth century Asians struggling to be free were the national movements in Italy and Ireland. The autobiographies of Asian politicians frequently recall a youthful enthusiasm for the Italian Risorgimento, the long, bitter struggle against Austrian domination. The story to which young Asians turned was not that of Cavour, the careful statesman, nor even that of Garibaldi, the Liberal Romantic, but to that of Mazzini : a story of high idealism, of youthful sacrifice, of secret societies and secret oaths, of plots, bombs, assassinations, armed risings. From his reading the excited Bengali student went forth to plan the murder of the local British District Judge. The atmosphere of the Irish struggle was equally perfervid ; the Fenians and dynamite, the Land League, rick burning and cattle maiming ; political murder, boycott, the disruption of the House of Commons by the exploitation of the rules of procedure so as to plunge the government of Britain into deadlock. The Irish example was especially potent to Indian and Burmese students in Britain ; and in Mrs. Annie Besant, Ireland sent an emissary to India who spread the technique of boycott, and urged the Indian National Congress to abandon constitutional agitation in favour of physical force. The effects of this education in violence may be read in the subsequent political history of India and Burma, from 1919 down to the achievement of independence. Defiance of authority, the wrecking of the Dyarchy parliamentary experiment, unrest in schools and colleges. And the lesson is not, even today, forgotten : in contemporary India, Pakistan and Burma, student strikes and hooliganism, political riot, political intimidation, the wrecking of public property are everyday occurrences.[15]

The last major European influence is, of course, that of Communism. Marx himself thought about the future of Asia within his philosophy of social and economic change. He contributed to the *New York Tribune* between 1852 and 1859, and among his articles were several dealing with India. Writing in the issue of August 8, 1853, before the impact of the first cotton mill or railway, he predicted the effects of railway development and industrialisation on India, culminating in the dissolution of caste. 'England,' he wrote, 'has to fulfil a double mission in India : one destructive, the other regenerating—the annihilating of old Asiatic society and the laying the material foundation of Western society in Asia.' Marx's concept of Britain's 'mission' conforms to his general thesis : the English 'moneyocracy' and 'millocracy' will exploit India 'till in Great Britain itself the now ruling classes shall have been supplanted by the industrial proletariat, or till the Hindoos themselves shall have grown strong enough to throw off the English yoke altogether.'

This concentration upon economic exploitation (in contrast to the American emphasis upon the denial of civil and political liberties) was taken further by J. A. Hobson in his *Imperialism : a Study,* published in the disillusioned aftermath of the Chamberlain era (1902). He examined why and how colonies became a necessary adjunct to capitalism in its search for investment and exploitation. This argument was made use of by Lenin in his work, *Imperialism, the Highest Stage of Capitalism,* published in 1916. Lenin foretold that the final phase of capitalism would

[15] Cf. J. Hennessy, *India, Democracy and Education,* 1955, Chapter 3.

be when 'The territorial division of the world by the greatest
capitalist powers is completed.' Whatever temporary agreements
might be observed by the imperialist powers, he envisaged an
ultimate conflict, leading to world revolution.

And so the Asian intellectual was provided with an economic
diagnosis of colonialism which dovetailed into his own observa-
tions. The Indian who held that the Indian cotton-weaving
industry had been deliberately killed for the benefit of Lancashire
looms; the Chinese who viewed the record of 'gunboat
diplomacy' carried on to prise open the doors of China to
European and American trade; the Javanese with his memories
of the Dutch Culture System and the forced deliveries of export
crops by the peasants of Java for the benefit of the Netherlands,
all found in the doctrine of Marx and Lenin the confirmation
of their own beliefs.

The Communist International Programme of 1928 pointed
to the conclusion of this process: 'Imperialism is capitalism
moribund and decaying. It is the final stage of development of
the capitalist system. It is the threshold of world social revolution.' 'Simultaneously, the antagonisms between the imperialist
home countries and the semi-colonial countries are growing. . . .
The great Chinese revolution, which roused hundreds of millions
of the Chinese people to action, caused an enormous breach in the
imperialist system. The unceasing ferment among hundreds of
millions of Indian workers and peasants is threatening to break the
world citadel of imperialism, Great Britain.' The Communist
International proceeded to lay down, among fundamental tasks of
the proletarian dictatorship: 'The recognition of the rights of all
nations, irrespective of race, to complete self-determination. . . .
Complete equality for all nations and races. . . . Every assistance
to be rendered to the economic, political and cultural growth of
the former oppressed "colonies" with the object of transferring
them to Socialist lines.' The liberal, humanitarian terms in
which the Communist programme was presented to the colonial
peoples helps to explain the appeal which Communism made to
the liberal-minded Asian intelligentsia.

Perhaps even more attractive was the image which was

impressed upon Asian thought by the Russian example. Not only did the Soviet Constitution appear to extend full citizenship and national self-determination to the Soviet Asian republics (including the right of secession from the U.S.S.R.!), but perhaps even more important, Russia appeared to provide an answer to the problem of social and economic rebirth with which Asian radicals were wrestling. They saw that before they could attain parity with Western nations they must carry out an economic revolution; they must transform peasant agriculture, raise its capacity from an almost 'subsistence' level to one of efficient crop yields; they must develop industry, including heavy industry, to become independent of Western capitalism. To do all this they must overhaul society, educate the peasant, eliminate the absentee landlord, and in place of the credit system of the 'parasitic' moneylender they must create a dynamic credit system capable of financing national development schemes. In the 1920s and 30s, British Conservatism and American Republicanism seemed to have succeeded in creating only mass unemployment and a world slump whose effects were keenly felt in the primary producing countries of Southern Asia. But Russian Communism did seem to supply an answer: it furnished solid evidence that a feudal society of landlords, kulaks and serfs could be transformed within a brief space into a modern industrialised, rational social order. If the Russian achievement appears to the Western reader as an empire of steelworks and collective farms raised upon the bones of hundreds of thousands of victims, he is asked to recall the Asian peasant and his patch of parched land, with his yearly struggle for survival, or the graduate clerk and his starveling wage. Democracy has no meaning to such as these unless political freedom demonstrably yields economic betterment: unless this is so, in desperation, the clerk or peasant will accept the regimentation of Communism in the hope of ultimate benefit.[16]

These, then, are the Western models which Asia copied and adapted to her own problems. But in the newly independent

---

[16] For a brief but stimulating exposition of the meaning of democracy in political, legal and economic terms, see D. Thomson, *Equality*, 1949.

countries, when political dogma is expounded in speeches or writing, it is not the precepts of Western political thinkers that are quoted, but, in India, the thoughts of Gandhi or Tilak; in Pakistan, the views of Jinnah or Iqbal; in Burma, the utterances of Aung San; in Indonesia, the sayings of Sukarno; in China, the pronouncements of Mao Tse-tung or Sun Yat-sen. It is an Asian version of Western democracy that now confronts the peoples of Asia.

Two of the most influential synthesists may be compared, Gandhi and Sun Yat-sen. Gandhi stepped into the centre of a political stage which had previously been dominated by two men : Gokhale and Tilak. Gokhale had accepted the 'Western' approach to liberal, representative institutions, education and social reform.[17] Tilak, a considerable student of the *Vedas*, the sacred writings of the Aryans, looked back to ancient Hindu India, regarding both Muslims and British as intruders who should be ejected. Gandhi was for a period a follower of Gokhale, but he is often regarded as the political heir of Tilak. Misled by Gandhi's cult of the *charka*, the Indian spinning wheel, his mode of life in the *ashram* at Wardha, writers have characterised Gandhi's philosophy as Hindu to the core. But Gandhi drew as much from other sources as from Hinduism : from Tolstoy, from Ruskin, from the Sermon on the Mount. Among Indian teachers he was particularly indebted to Swami Vivekananda, whose Hinduism laid greatest stress upon renunciation (or saintliness) and social service, reaching down to the centre of religious experience.[18] Inspired by Vivekananda, Gandhi continually emphasised the contribution of Asian thought to the world : he overcame the 'slave mentality,' the inferiority complex of colonial Asia towards a superior Europe. He clothed his ideas in a Hindu guise, because his appeal was not to the Westernised minority, but to the tradition-moulded millions. *Satyagraha* (literally 'sacrifice-firmness,' but usually translated 'soul-force') was a technique of civil disobedience, the passive breaking of the

[17] But in the Servants of India Society, Gokhale created an organisation that was uniquely Indian.
[18] From time to time the Swami would set aside periods in which he would endeavour to think, live, feel, as a Buddhist, or a Muslim, or a Christian.

law, such as Gandhi's making of salt from brine in defiance of
the salt regulations : *satyagraha* was not really a traditional
Hindu concept, but as presented by Gandhi it was accepted into
the broad stream of Hindu custom. Similarly, *ahimsa*, harmless-
ness, or non-violence, was not an essential attribute of orthodox
Hinduism : Tilak, Lala Lajpat Rai, Subhas Chandra Bose, and
other leaders stressed the heroic, challenging, sacrificing, con-
quering traditions of Hinduism.[19] Some of Gandhi's teachings
were, indeed, anathema to orthodox Hindus; such were his
advocacy of women's rights, or his campaign against untoucha-
bility; but by replying to his Hindu critics upon Hindu lines,
Gandhi succeeded in keeping the support of even such champions
of orthodoxy as Pandit Madan Mohan Malaviya. However, in
the end it was a member of a Right-wing Hindu organisation who
assassinated Gandhi.

Whenever Gandhi failed to persuade his followers to follow
the path of non-violence, from the slaughter of the police at
Chauri Chaura in 1921, down to the 'August Disturbances' of
1942, his cause failed. Paradoxically, the authorities could
always put down riot and rebellion but they were disarmed by
non-violence. Gandhi's numerous political fasts (another un-
orthodox extension of Hindu custom) when he threatened nothing
except his own life rocked New Delhi and Westminster. Gandhi's
moral triumphs included that of weakening the confidence of
British administrators in their mission of trusteeship, so that, in
the end, power was transferred not so much because British statesmen had become convinced that India was ready for this step,
nor because Britain was unable to hold on any longer, but mainly
because British politicians and officials came to feel that it was
no longer morally justifiable to withhold independence from a
people whose demand was so ardent and so cogent. But an
essential condition for the success of Gandhi's mission was the
existence of the Rule of Law. Gandhi and his followers defied
and denied the authority of the British Government of India,
but they relied upon exploiting freedom of assembly, freedom of

[19] *Bande Mataram,* India's national song was, in its original context, the
marching song of a band of Hindu patriots, fighting and defeating the
Muslim oppressor.

speech and of the press. When they broke the law they refused
to plead when brought before the courts: but they expected
to enjoy the rights of an accused person in an English court of
law. Non-violence worked: but only because the opponent
observed his self-imposed rules. A certain contrast is provided
by the failure of post-independence Indian attempts to subvert
Portuguese authority in Goa by passive disobedience. The
government of Goa replied to the 'non-violent' invasion of
Indian *satyagrahis* by employing force, and more force, until
the invasion was abandoned. *Satyagraha* against Goa was called
off, and the technique has not been employed there again.

While we must acclaim the Gandhian synthesis as the
apotheosis of Indian nationalism, we should also observe that
its fulfilment emerged from the assimilation of English constitutional principles into the British-Indian government system.

By comparison, Sun Yat-sen attempted to reform or revolu-
tionise a China which, despite the incursions of the West, had
remained largely unchanged in its intellectual climate and its
system of government. Whereas in India and Ceylon, British
ideas and institutions made a wide impact in the sphere of
government and political thought, in China Western pressure,
although heavy and sustained, was insulated from the main
stream of Chinese life. For example, the Western Powers
obtained territorial concessions in the ports of which the greatest
was Shanghai. Here a community of over one million lived
in the International Settlement run by a British-style munici-
pality, within the ambit of Western law, commerce, journalism
and other influences. But whereas in India, Bombay and
Calcutta provided an important training-ground for democracy,
Shanghai was no kind of lighthouse to China: rather, it was a
constant reminder of the humiliations which had been imposed
upon the Middle Kingdom by the Foreign Devils. The Western
universities established in the eastern provinces by American
missions, were also largely insulated from Chinese life and
thought. Western higher education was sought after in India
partly because it was the key to a career in the higher civil
service or at the Bar: but in China, until the last years of the

Empire, entry into the civil service was restricted to scholars proficient in the Confucian classics. Western education did not, as it were, construct a bridge across society through its absorption by the higher administration. Recent research has laid stress on the efforts made by successive reformers working within the Imperial Chinese administration to adapt institutions and ideas to meet the challenge of the outside world : but these efforts were defeated by a series of disasters. The China of the early twentieth century remained the old China.

Part of Gandhi's success was due to his appeal to the Indian masses as a figure from tradition, an ascetic, a holy man, *mahatma*. Sun lived wholly outside the Chinese tradition. He was educated at Western schools and colleges, he professed himself a Christian, he was utterly opposed to the Confucian view of society; he was an outlaw under the Imperial regime being compelled to live outside China, in Japan and South East Asia, and he drew most of his support from the expatriate Chinese of the *Nan Yang* (Southern Seas). He was obliged to attack the old order from the periphery, by encouraging risings by his supporters. But like Mazzini he was a dreamer not a realist and no less than ten of his plots failed. When, in 1911, the Empire finally collapsed, Sun Yat-sen returned from overseas and in December was elected President of the Provisional Republic of China. These events, seen through Western spectacles, are usually labelled the Chinese Revolution; but in fact there was no revolution, no sudden, forcible replacement of one system of government by another, radically different; instead, the fabric of Chinese government disintegrated into anarchy. Traditional order was replaced by traditional disorder : the rule of the Warlords.[20]

[20] The relative significance attributed to Sun and Gandhi in Marxist dogma is curious. The following extract is taken from the Programme of the Communist International, 1928: 'Sun Yat-senism in China expressed the ideology of petty-bourgeois democratic "socialism" . . . While it played a very useful role in the first stage of the Chinese revolution, as a consequence of the further process of class differentiation . . . Sun-Yat-senism has now changed from being the ideological expression of that revolution into fetters of its further development.' 'Tendencies like Gandhism in India, thoroughly imbued with religious conceptions, idealise the most reactionary forms of social life . . . Gandhism is more and more becoming an ideology directed against mass revolution. It must be strongly combated by Communism.'

Sun's *Kuo Ming Tang,* 'People's Party,' only became an effective political force under his successor, Chiang Kai-shek, but inasmuch as the KMT possessed a political philosophy it was derived from Sun. The Western influence that appears most obviously in his writings is that of Henry George the American nineteenth century political economist who propounded the theory that all economic problems would be solved by his form of land tax. Sun was attracted at various times by the political institutions of France, the United States and Britain; but he finally reached the conclusion that it would be necessary to devise a special form of government for China. He therefore propounded the *San Min Chu I* or 'Three People's Principles,' which were Nationalism, Socialism and Democracy. His Nationalism owed something, perhaps, to President Wilson; but it derived mainly from Chinese exclusiveness, contempt for the foreigner, whether Westerner or Manchu. The Socialist principle reflected Sun's interest in George's Land Tax; the Democracy emphasised control by the electorate over the government; but the constitution which Sun devised was more authoritarian than democratic. This Five-fold Constitution divided the government into five parts: besides the familiar separation of powers into Legislative, Judicial and Executive, there was to be a division called the 'Examining Power,' which was to provide the public services, and a 'Censorate' or 'Control Power' to provide a check on officials and on the public. The scheme bears the mark of Chinese logical thinking, and in some details (notably the Examining Power and the Censorate) followed Chinese patterns: but it was a constitution in a vacuum, and amid the difficulties of the 1920s the constitution went by default. What was its contribution, and that of its author, compared to that of Gandhi in India?

Gandhi gave his countrymen faith and confidence to wage the struggle for independence: but in shaping the actual form of government for independent India he had absolutely no share. India gradually absorbed and adapted a wide range of Western institutions of government and, by 1947, sufficient officials, politicians and others were trained in the working of these institutions to make independence a practical reality. Gandhi was able to carry on his 'experiments with truth' upon a moral plane, while others of his countrymen worked out vital issues on levels of practical politics or practical administration.[1] Sun Yat-sen, by comparison, attempted to devise new theories of government for China which were alien to the national genius. His Western-style constitutional innovations made little practical contribution to national regeneration. The KMT political theorists produced no less than six constitutions between 1912 and 1925, and meanwhile, the mandarins and the Warlords held sway and power was all. An expatriate, working most of his life out of touch with the pulse of China, Sun could not build up his movement into a national rally receiving the support (even if it was only passive support) of the millions. This was where Sun failed : the 'filtration' of ideas from an intelligentsia out through the masses never took place : indeed, there was no sort of emotional identification between the KMT party and the mass of the people.[2] The KMT never developed a coherent, national political philosophy and words like 'parliament' or 'democracy,' so far as they were ever used, remained abstractions, foreign and meaningless. The ordinary Chinese peasant only knew that the old, stable Imperial government was gone, the Mandate of Heaven had lapsed. And now there were hard men who wrung additional taxes from the peasant, or conscripted his sons, in the name of the People's Party : but what People, or what Party, he did not understand.

> 'Oh, wearisome condition of humanity,
> Born under one law, to another bound.'

The importance of the manner in which democracy comes to the Asian masses is now, perhaps, more clear. If it is presented as having some connection with his own thought and

---

[1] Perhaps some comparison with Gladstone is possible. Gladstone, in his old age, compelled his party and his country to focus their attentions upon a series of moral issues, culminating in Irish Home Rule. He ignored many issues posed by social reform, problems of industry and trade, and imperialism, which he left to a later generation of politicians to solve.

[2] Sun also lacked such practical facilities as a railway network, telegraph services, printing presses, road transport, which in India made possible Gandhi's nation-wide campaigns.

custom, and if it is backed by a stable government system, then
democracy may take hold of the mind of the ordinary man,
as it has in Gandhi's India. But if democracy is foisted upon a
people, foreign and unassimilated, as a panacea, political peni-
cillin, warranted to cure all social ills; and if it manifestly does
not promote stability and public order, then it will fail, as it
failed in Sun Yat-sen's China. And perhaps the failure of this
phoney democracy will damn the real thing, leaving the way
open for a more compulsive creed, Communism.

Up to this point, we have dwelt largely upon the process
whereby democracy has made its impact upon the mind of Asia.
The actual working of the democratic system is so limited in
duration that any dogmatic conclusions concerning the success
or failure of the idea in Asia are clearly premature. The first
country to advance along this path was Ceylon, which adopted
universal franchise for men and women over twenty-one in 1931,
only three years after its introduction in Great Britain, and many
years in advance of a number of politically mature Western
countries. But Ceylon did not attain full independence until
February 1948. Malaya, the last of the major colonial territories in East Asia to acquire independence, hoisted the flag of
Merdeka, Freedom, in August 1957, but remains a long way
from conceding universal franchise to all the inhabitants of
Malaya.[3] Siam, nominally a constitutional monarchy since
1932, has yet to hold its first free election. Japan acquiesced
in the reception of democratic institutions from 1945 onwards,
but few would agree that conditions under which the people
can exercise a free choice have yet arrived. All the Asian democratic countries are virtually at the start of their journey: an
observer can do little more than indicate some influences that
will affect future developments.

Nationalism, or national consciousness, is something which in
Britain is taken entirely for granted; but in Asia it is brand new,
and it is full of emotional surprises. In times past, the Asian,
whether of the upper or the lower classes, has felt himself identi-

---

[3] British Borneo and Hongkong, Dutch New Guinea, American Okinawa,
Portuguese Timor, Macao and Goa remain under colonial rule: but
these are all special cases.

fied with a unit smaller than the nation : a linguistic area, a
tribe or caste, a district, a town, or a village has represented
'home' or mother-earth, and all who shared this 'home' were
brothers. There were exceptions : among the great nations,
the Chinese, and among the small, the Burmese have always been
conscious of their identity with their country. But the Chinese
did not regard the non-Chinese-speaking peoples of the Chinese
Empire—Mongols, Tai, Turki, and many others—as fellow-
nationals; nor did the Burmese regard the non-Burmese-speaking
Karens, Chins or Kachins as 'Burmans.' Only in one country
was national identity equated with the nation-state; the country
where the Imperial State was elevated into a national religion;
Japan.

During the movements for independence, the middle classes
everywhere came to identify themselves with the nation; and
yet many still feel the emotional pull of older, smaller group-
loyalties; the peasant millions have, to a lesser degree, come to
regard themselves as part of the nation. It is relatively easy to
convince people that they are Indians if they are emotionally
roused against their British overlords, and the same with Indo-
nesians under the Dutch, or Vietnamese under the French, but
the emotional position becomes less simple when independence
is attained. In almost every country in Southern Asia there are
opposed loyalties, nationalism against regionalism, and a satis-
factory solution of this conflict is essential to the functioning of
a democratic State. In India, the problem has been tackled on
federal lines by the creation of linguistic states, a major operation
in political surgery. Certain groups have not been appeased
by the formula adopted, notably the Sikhs and the Nagas, but
in general the central government has produced acceptable solutions, and has checkmated Communist attempts to exploit local
loyalties. In Ceylon, where independence was achieved without
recourse to violence or bitterness, the dispute between the Sin-
halese-speaking majority and the Tamil-speaking minority
threatens, for the first time, to introduce bloodshed into politics.
In Burma, the discontent of the second largest community, the
Karens, boiled up into civil war, while leaders of the Shans talk

somewhat wildly of secession. In Indonesia, the pull of regional loyalties has, apparently, in 1957, brought this State of a thousand islands to the point of dissolution. In Malaya the problem of uniting the Malays and Chinese in a true Malayan nationhood remains unsolved on the threshold of independence and may well wreck the Malayan State before real nationhood is attained. Only a fool would underestimate the fissiparous forces which the new nations have to overcome in creating a true national patriotism. But the picture is not all darkness. There are devoted men in most of the new countries who put nation above group. And there are forces which contribute towards national awareness: the *esprit de corps* of the higher civil service and the army; trade unions and national political parties; radio, and other means of easier communication. All these are working to create common attitudes and a common national feeling.

If the nation-state is threatened by regionalism in one direction, it is threatened in another by the claims of religion. A major new factor in the world today is the revival of Islam as an international force. Pakistan is a unique expression of the Islamic tenet that the believer cannot accept the rule of an unbeliever (*Dar-ul-Harb*) when it is possible to create by struggle an Islamic State (*Dar-ul-Islam*). It should certainly not be assumed that liberal Muslim politicians such as Jinnah accepted the inevitability of conflict in this way: Jinnah always declared that he was driven to demand a separate Muslim State because of the intolerance of the Hindu majority, and he certainly did not intend that the State of his creation should be theocratic. But Islam, a fighting religion, a brotherhood of believers, does not appear to accommodate itself easily to the Western concept of a polity where State and religion are separated, where law and civil liberty are outside the orbit of Faith. In every Asian country where Muslims are numerous there is pressure to associate religion with political decision. In Pakistan there is pressure to make Acts of Parliament subject to review by the *Ulama* learned in theology. Indonesia has its *Dar-ul-Islam* movement, banned by the government, which carries on a guerrilla war for

a purely Islamic State.   Malaya is witnessing strong efforts to
give the Muslim religion a special place in the new constitution.
But it is not only Islam which poses the problem of religion in
politics.   Militant Hinduism has not fared well in attempts to
build up a political platform in India, but it is too early to say
positively that it has no future.   The determined stand of Pandit
Nehru for a secular State, and the command which he possesses
over the nation, have checked the *Mahasabha,* the *Jan Sangh,*
and other religious parties, but they can still look to a formidable
reservoir of orthodox Hindu feeling.   Buddhism, after centuries
of quiescence, has again become a missionary religion and the
meeting of the Sixth Great Buddhist Council at Rangoon from
1954–56 was a remarkable international assemblage.   Buddhism
appeared as an issue in the 1956 Ceylon Elections; it is a potent
force in Burmese politics, somewhat masked because U Nu has
successfully canalised its influence into support of the coalition
government.   In Siam, Laos and Cambodia, where politics is as
yet a species of ritual game, it represents a latent source of political energy.   At the least, any politician bidding for popular
support would have to tailor his programme upon a Buddhist
pattern.

An entirely separate problem, one by no means peculiar to
Asia even if especially acute there, is the reconciliation of
democracy with State direction of economic and social activity.
Democracy is an idea evolved in a phase of history when the
impact of the State upon the individual was largely confined to
the maintenance of law and order.   Today, the individual has to
accept the interference of the community in the greater part of
his activities : how can this be controlled by parliament and the
other organs of public opinion?   In Asia, the new States are concerned to push through schemes of economic development to
expand productive capacity.   In this massive, urgent planning
and building by the State, the role of democracy is far from clear.
In Britain the problem of effective public control over nation-
alised industries has only been fiddled with : in the newly
independent Asian countries there is a grave danger that this
kind of problem will go by default.   The needs of the State will

always be more important than liberty.   Can democracy, squeezed into a corner, so to speak, survive?

Democracy has to face its greatest test in Asia, and it is most likely that in some countries its final metamorphosis will bear little resemblance to anything known in the West.   But in those countries where a certain synthesis between East and West has been achieved, the establishment of a genuine, Asian democracy can be awaited with a measure of confidence.

VI
DEMOCRATIC INSTITUTIONS
IN
INDIA AND CHINA

VI

DEMOCRATIC INSTITUTIONS IN INDIA AND CHINA

HUGH TINKER

THE title of this chapter may seem a notable piece of question-begging; democratic institutions in India—perhaps; but in China—certainly not. As Professor C. H. Philips has pointed out, China's much-discussed revolution was, in fact, the replacement of one authoritarian regime by another, whereas India's new constitution represents a complete departure from former Indian models, a genuine attempt to transform the national attitude to politics and society.[1] Nevertheless, the title chosen is not 'all vanity . . . wind and confusion': in Asia today, there are two countries which shine as twin stars, to which the gaze of all the emergent countries is drawn, whether eagerly or reluctantly. After more than a century of impotence and apparent subservience, these two nations have taken their stand as giants upon the world scene, and will certainly loom larger as the twentieth century merges into the twenty-first. Looking at India, the *Manchester Guardian* observed, 'Parliamentary institutions have not had a very good time in Asia . . . [However] Pericles said that Athens was the school of Hellas. Mr. Nehru without boasting may say that Delhi is the school of Asia.'[2] Peking offers an attraction of another order: not parliamentary democracy, but a Peoples' Democracy is here on show to Asia. It was argued in the previous chapter that while the idea of liberty and free institutions may be important to a small

---

[1] C. H. Philips, 'Tradition and Experiment in Asia,' B.B.C. Home Service, February-March 1954.
[2] June 5, 1954. Quoted by W. H. Morris-Jones in *Parliament in India*, p. 327. The point of view adopted in this chapter has been evolving in the writer's mind over many years, but Professor Morris-Jones's important work has been much in consideration during the actual writing of these pages. *Parliament in India* is by far the most comprehensive analysis of the structure and working of an Asian system of democracy.

number of thinking, Westernised Asians, to the majority the most important consideration is the reduction of a poverty which is never far from starvation, with opportunity for the under-privileged, including many of the poorly-paid educated classes, and the abolition of gross inequality; inequality as between nations, and as between man and man. In all these matters, China points the way with sonorous call and steady march. The democracy of equality confronts the democracy of liberty, and the outcome of this tacit, far from openly-admitted rivalry is likely to determine the course of Asian history, and perhaps that of the world.

In this essay the writer is attempting to interpret Asian attitudes to Western readers, but it is necessary to relate Asian evolution to an absolute, 'the democratic ideal,' and to attempt to measure the development of India and China against this somewhat intangible idea. China, which created one of the first systematic and standardised systems of government in the world, has perpetuated this system almost unchanged into modern times. India, by contrast, has traditionally been much less con-cerned with the relationship of the individual to government than with the place of man in a quasi-religious society of caste custom and government. Indian thought was concerned in the past not so much with 'political man' as with 'socio-religious man.' (to coin a fearful phrase). Present-day attempts in India to liqui-date religious restrictions upon social relations, and to link the individual with the State through political processes, represent a radical innovation. Whatever reservations the observer may wish to make about some aspects of Indian democracy, he is compelled to acknowledge that the transformation in thinking already accomplished is so striking that anticipation of future political advance and consolidation falls into the field of sober expectation rather than that of reckless surmise.

We have already had to notice the narrow base from which the attempt was made to build democracy in China; democratic institutions, in consequence, virtually never established themselves. Under the Imperial regime, nationalist reformers had no means of acquiring familiarity with the working of these institutions from the inside : they could not even enjoy the limited opportunities open to the Indian National Congress to learn the political facts of life which were obtained by its annual sessions from 1885 onwards, for open political agitation was impossible in the Chinese Empire. The reformers had, perforce, to adopt the model of the 'Secret Societies' which were such a feature of Chinese life : part benefit club, part protection racket. And so they plotted in their secret meetings, scratching around the problem of how to build up an armed force with which to seize and hold power : their activities were worlds away from that of the Indian Congress with its public debates and resolutions by vote.

With the sudden collapse of the old order in 1911, Sun Yat-sen's followers, the KMT, as the only coherent party, took the lead in stating political objectives and in setting up a provisional (self-appointed) national assembly. But the only forces available to give effect to their plans were those controlled by the mandarins of the former regime. The attempt of the KMT to enlist the support of the most powerful of these, Yuan Shih-k'ai, was disastrous. Yuan was elected President, and with the backing of the most powerful army in China he dismissed the national assembly and made a bid to restore the Empire with himself as Emperor; the attempt failed, and Yuan is supposed, subsequently, to have been 'liquidated'; he died in 1916. Thereafter, different factions laid their claims to represent the Government of China, but China had in fact become a 'geographical expression.'[3] Provinces and cities were ruled by Warlords, mainly former mandarins, but some merely successful bandits. During this phase, law and government ceased to exist : might was right, and the ruler was he who was most powerful and pitiless. Despair was everywhere, among the former official classes, among the Western-educated advocates of democracy, and most of all among the peasants; pillaged, enslaved, powerless. All this while Japan was exerting pressure upon her great neighbour, extending her grip on Manchuria, planning to con-

[3] Cf. Linebarger, Djang Chu, and Burks, *Far Eastern Government and Politics*, 1954, p. 121. 'The first Chinese republic was a foreign office attached to domestic chaos.'

vert the whole of China into a satellite. And the coastal towns, occupied by the Marines and gunboats of America, Britain and France were virtually Western colonies. The cup of China's misery and humiliation was brimful.

Two movements offered a hope for the future: a newly founded Communist Party, and the KMT, revitalised under Chiang Kai-shek. Both these groups in their struggle with domestic reactionaries and foreign imperialists drew upon connections overseas, with America and Russia. An important element in the KMT was provided by American-educated Chinese of the commercial class, of whom the Soong family are the most important and best known. This group was small but highly influential: its members were mostly educated in American missionary schools and universities, many of them were Christians, some for purposes of convenience only. Almost all were connected with business interests, import-export houses, or manufactures. A feature of the Eastern coastal provinces was the number of Americans born in China of missionary parents, perhaps second or third generation China-born, who were also engaged in business. Here was one of the ties between the KMT and the important American China missionary 'lobby' which was greatly to influence happenings in the 1930s and 40s. During the 1920s a much more potent force was that of the Soviet Union. From the earliest days of the November Revolution, the Russian Communists amid their many perplexities set themselves the task of wooing China. In 1919 they announced 'The Soviet Government returns to the Chinese people without demanding any compensation, the Chinese Eastern Railway, as well as the mining concessions, forestry, gold mines, and all other things which were seized from them by the government of the Czar . . .' It is true that the Russians were only making a gesture, giving up things they did not possess, and that the final agreement signed in May 1924 left the Russians considerable control over the Eastern Railway: but to the Chinese, the contrast offered to the demands of the West was agreeable. The Soviet attitude to the upheavals in China, as enunciated by Lenin, was that 'We as Communists must and will support

bourgeois emancipation movements in the colonial countries
. . .' and he distinguished two stages of revolution, the first 'the
bourgeois-democratic revolution with the agrarian movement as
its principal axis, and the second stage, . . . the capture of
power by the proletariat.' And so, Russian influence was directed
both towards the KMT and the Chinese Communists.

The Communist movement originated in a study-group of
teachers and students at Peking University who met to discuss
Marxism: among these students was Mao Tse-tung. The
Chinese Communist Party was founded in 1921 by Ch'en
Tu-hsiu, a Peking University professor who was expelled from
the Party a few months later. While support came almost entirely from intellectuals, work began amongst the few trade
unions existing in the ports, and in 1925 extensive strikes were
staged in Shanghai and Hongkong. Communist activities did
not seem to compare in importance with those of the KMT.
During his last years, Sun Yat-sen was drawn towards Communist
ideology, largely under the suggestion of Michael Borodin and
Adolphe Joffe. His successor, Chiang Kai-shek, was a man of
action rather than a political thinker. Trained at the Tokyo
Staff College, his great foundation was the Whampoa Military
Academy, an officers' training school which was staffed largely
by members of a Soviet Military Mission led by General Blücher
(alias Galen). From this institution were to come the leaders of
the KMT armies and many KMT administrators—and, by a
curious paradox—many of the Communist generals and other
leaders who later supplanted them. The keynote was a fiercely
Chinese, anti-foreign spirit, but Chiang was quite prepared, at
first, to make use of Russian help: he spent some time in Russia,
and he sent his eldest son, Chiang Ching-kuo, to Moscow for his
education.

Russian policy towards China was confused in the 1920s, and
some notable dialectical tussles took place between Stalin and his
opponents, Trotsky, Zinoviev, Kamenev, and others. The
theoretical position was clear enough: the Communist International Programme, adopted at the Sixth Congress in 1928,
stated plainly that in 'Colonial and semi-colonial countries

(China, India, etc.). . . . The principal task . . . is, on the one hand, to fight against the feudal and pre-capitalist forms of exploitation, and to develop systematically the peasant agrarian revolution; on the other, to fight against foreign imperialism.' This represents a shrewd enough forecast of what was to come in China, but neither Stalin nor his opponents were clear about the actual application of this doctrine. If events in China represented an agrarian revolution, then this was the period of the 'national bourgeoisie,' the time for Communism was not yet ripe: when the moment came to break with the bourgeois-socialist group, then the struggle must be waged chiefly by the urban proletariat, in the 'Soviet stage of revolution.' Stalin is usually supposed to have blundered, to have continued to back the KMT until Mao's peasants had, by their own unaided efforts, achieved the revolution. The actual course of events was far more complex. During the early 1920s the Communists co-operated with the KMT with the object of utilising a 'united front' to infiltrate into the KMT organisation. The Communist Party became a constituent part of the KMT in 1923, and Communists attained key positions, notably in the KMT agrarian and labour organisations. But Chiang Kai-shek was too powerful to be overcome by these tactics. Differences between the 'Right wing' KMT under Chiang and the 'Left wing' together with the Communists came into the open at the Second KMT Congress in January 1926. The two elements played along together for a little longer, but Chiang was denounced by the Comintern for his 'treacherous and reactionary policy'; the Communists intensified their efforts to overthrow 'the counter-revolution.'[4] Chiang rallied his Right-wing supporters, attacked the Communists, seized the records of the Russian Embassy and, despite setbacks, went on to bring most of China under his authority by 1928.

At this time the crying need of the ordinary Chinese was for 'Freedom from Fear' and 'Freedom from Want.' These seemed

---

[4] A speech by Stalin to the Central Committee of the Communist Party of the U.S.S.R. delivered on August 1, 1927, was devoted to the China controversy. It shows that Stalin was aware that China represented, in many ways, a separate problem from that of Russia.

to be promised by Chiang's regime : everywhere it was said that his soldiers abstained from looting, his officials were incorrupt, and the writ of the Central Government was observed. Sun Yat-sen's concept of 'controlled democracy' was officially adopted, together with his five-fold division of government. A new era seemed about to be born.

Within a few years all was dark again; and the principal cause was the pressure of Japan. In September 1931 Japan effectively seized control over Manchuria; war between the two nations did not formally commence until 1937, but henceforth Chiang and his associates were immersed in the struggle for survival. The strain of unending conflict against enemies external and internal was too much for the KMT Government. The ever-expanding Japanese blockade dislocated trade, pushed up prices, created shortages. Along with uncontrolled inflation came the black-market, and there were officials and politicians ready to use their power to exploit the opportunities created by these twin evils. Japanese military operations, although not in themselves damaging, severed the always tenuous communications of the sub-continent. Armies had to be mobilised to check these advances and revenues raised to pay for them. Governors and other officials who may originally have been patriotic, enlightened men, became hard and cynical after years of improvisation, of wringing taxes from a parched population, of isolation from the central government. Peasant soldiers dragged away from their fields, marched a thousand miles to fight an enemy infinitely better armed, organised and led, became demoralised, trigger-happy, as one defeat and retreat followed another. And the KMT which had raised the flag of national regeneration was stigmatised with the responsibility for all this corruption and demoralisation.

Paradoxically, as the KMT regime (largely for reasons outside its control) sank ever lower in the estimation of the people of China, so it rose ever higher in the esteem of the outside world, particularly in that of the United States. Fostered by the missionary connection, and skilfully exploited by the efforts of American-educated KMT propagandists, a legend grew of

Chiang Kai-shek as a great liberal Christian statesman, and of
the KMT regime as a western-style democracy.[5] China's struggle
with militarist Japan seemed to mark her as the champion of
democracy against fascism. Some of the Indian nationalist
leaders joined in this international admiration, among them
Nehru and Rajagopalacharya. These Indian nationalists identified their own struggle with a foreign 'invader' (Britain) with
what they saw as a similar nationalist uprising by China against
the Japanese invader. And so, the China of 1937–45 became
the cynosure of ardent democrats both in Asia and the West.

What was the reality? At best, the KMT Government was
authoritarian, a one party state. Not only was the opposition
illegal, but preferment in the administration, the army, or big
business was given only to prominent party members; and
increasingly the KMT adopted totalitarian methods; there was
a rigid censorship, and a powerful security police, with special
'murder squads' who eliminated prominent critics or deviation-
ists. And while the world applauded China's struggle, in many
sectors the armies facing the Japanese forces seemed to competent foreign observers to spend their time in shadow-boxing,
contracting curious local armistices or making unexplained with-
drawals; and all the time, rumour said that American Lease-
Lend military material was being secretly stored away for the
eventual destruction of the Chinese Communists.

The Communists, the alternative focus of Chinese hopes,
were meanwhile tenaciously building up their strength. Whether
or not Mao Tse-tung was disavowed by the Comintern and by
Stalin as is commonly stated, his methods remained orthodox
Soviet methods. Despite the capture or killing of many Com-
munists by the KMT armies after the break of 1926–27, a
Soviet 'republic' was founded in Kiang-si province, north of
Canton. KMT pressure became steadily tighter until, in 1934,

[5] This writer finds it hard to accept all the implications of the theories
propounded by G. Gorer in *The Americans*, 1948. But his chapter
'Lesser Breeds' is very convincing: he points out that if a State is a
republic with a president it is accepted as therefore similar to the
American system and *ipso facto* democratic. He points out (p. 174)
that 'The Chinese have been the special recipients of this peculiar
form of flattery.'

the Communists burst through the encircling armies and made their epic 'Long March' across the borderland of China to Yenan in Shensi province. Here they created a rugged new State, their capital, caves in the mountainside; their land a desert; here they trained their cadres, built up their army, launched their programme of land nationalisation and peasant co-operative farming.

In December 1936 there occurred the strange incident of the kidnapping of Chiang by Left-wing KMT officers, his release, and an uneasy truce to the KMT/Communist civil war for the purpose of combating the Japanese. During the following years a few American liaison officers made contact with the Communists, and reports reached the outside world that were surely as misleading as the legend of the 'freedom-loving' KMT. The Communists were depicted as progressive agrarian reformers, almost like the Western prairie pioneers. Gradually the Communists increased their territory and expanded their following: an increase in party membership from 100,000 in 1937 to 1,200,000 in 1945 seems not unlikely. And all the while the KMT strength and hold upon the nation shrivelled away.

V.E. Day saw Chiang apparently at the height of his prestige, one of the Big Five, but the hollow nature of the position was soon exposed. Xenophobia and territorial ambition had been elements in the outlook of the KMT, and had been revealed to a considerable extent in Chiang's political testament, *China's Destiny*, published in 1943. In the immediate post-war period attempts were made to extend Chinese power and influence. Eyes were cast upon Hongkong and even upon Malaya. The reoccupation of Formosa was carried out with little consideration for its inhabitants. Chinese forces reappeared in northern Burma and claims were advanced to the vast jungle tracts to the north of Myitkyina. In Tongking attempts were made to oust the French from their colony; Chinese troops were withdrawn only after France had retroceded Kwang-Chou-Wan; Ho Chi Minh was given support as the head of a Vietnamese government of which, it was hoped, China would pull the strings. But this resumption of traditional Chinese expansionism was soon overlaid by the crisis resulting from the breakdown of the truce between the KMT and the Communists. Attempts were made by American emissaries to patch up further agreements, but these efforts were abandoned as useless by January 1947. Thereafter, the United States tried to prop up the crumbling KMT government, with diminishing success. One attempt was made to shore up the regime by giving it a semblance of popular support. In November 1946 a National Assembly was convened at Nanking: it was told that the 'one party' era was now to be terminated and to be replaced by a multi-party, democratic structure. Elections were held throughout the country in November 1947: there was considerable freedom in the electioneering and opposition elements came forward with proposals for reform: Sun Yat-sen's son and widow marshalled a considerable following. But the procedure of indirect election adopted favoured the KMT, and the more radical opposition parties were banned. In March 1948 the new National Assembly met at Nanking and, despite a display of reluctance, Chiang allowed himself to be elected President of the Republic. This feigned appeal to the people had little practical effect in checking the decline of the KMT's fortunes. The principle grievances of the people were the continuance of the wartime shortages and of rising prices. The ports were now open to the world and there was a considerable influx of UNRRA stores, but distribution arrangements were faulty and the supplies were frequently not suitable for Chinese requirements. Corruption and inflation became ever more gross and more out of control. As in Germany in the early 1920s, the middle class became demoralised by the swallowing up of savings and salaries in the uncontrolled flood of worthless paper money.

The Communists began their advance, and everywhere their forces were successful. Chiang commanded huge armies, but they became demoralised. Members of the American military advisory missions attempted to rally the disintegrating KMT forces, and by a rueful paradox the xenophobia generated by the KMT leaders was now directed at their American allies. American planes, tanks, guns, trucks, were poured in; American liaison officers advised Chiang's generals; American training teams attempted to conjure up new supplies of fighting men; American marines stood guard over key installations. The bitterness which was vented against the decaying KMT tyranny was turned upon the United States who, it was said, was trying to prop up the reactionaries : in the interests, of course, of Dollar Imperialism. As the Communists entered city after city and province after province they brought the same promise that had seemed to accompany the KMT in the late 1920s; an army that did not loot or riot; officials who were incorrupt, austere and efficient. And the Communists promised more : a plan for the control of inflation : a plan which in practice worked. There were other plans for land rationalisation and industrialisation : these were welcomed, but it was the ending of the inflation nightmare which chiefly made the Communists welcome to conservative peasants and the westernised, liberal intelligentsia.

By the last months of 1949 the Communist march was completed; the KMT was driven out over the Burma border and into the island fortress of Formosa. Democracy, as the free nations understand the term, had not received the barest trial in China : yet it was damned. Its entire message had been misapprehended. In its place was Communism on a Russian, Soviet model : acquiesced in, if not preferred, as the only way for China.

Eighteen months before the Communist/KMT struggle reached its climax another struggle almost equally seismic in character came to a conclusion : the British Empire of India was replaced by the independent states of India and Pakistan. This consummation also was not achieved without violence and bloodshed, yet it heralded the greatest declaration in favour of parliamentary democracy the world may ever see. What distinguishes India—and Pakistan—from China?[6] KMT China knew neither freedom nor good government; Communist China has achieved good government, but at the price of the suppression of individual liberty; India and Pakistan enjoy good government and, equally important, freedom, and government

[6] The plan of this book was not of the present writer's choosing and the virtual exclusion of Pakistan has been determined by problems of space rather than by doubts as to its standing as a parliamentary democracy.

according to law. To understand how this system has evolved, a study of political ideas and parties alone is not sufficient; account must also be taken (among other factors) of the civil service, the army, the system of education, the press and, most important of all, the judiciary and the law.

The Indian Civil Service developed over a period of 150 years, being made up of a small élite of a few hundreds, directing 'provincial' and 'subordinate' civil services. A significant point was reached in 1853 when a system of entry by open competition was introduced: the I.C.S. thus formed the model for the other higher civil services in Britain and other parts of the Commonwealth. Another milestone was passed in the 1920s with the accelerated 'Indianisation' of the élite civil service so that by the time of the transfer of power almost half the key posts were already held by Hindus and Muslims with an adequate reserve of trained men to step into the positions vacated by the departing British, thus ensuring a smooth take-over. The tradition built up during the British period has been carried on in independent India and Pakistan. What were its main features? Loyalty, to the State and to colleagues; unhesitating acceptance of responsibility; a working day that knew no 'office hours' and availability to the public, which involved long, leisurely tours through remote rural areas. This tradition has a less attractive side: a 'closed shop' attitude to outsiders, a certain mental arrogance and aloofness, a measure of contempt for politicians and others who dabble their fingers in dirt, a tendency to assume that the civil service always knows better than the public what is good. But these blemishes count for little compared to the benefit which has been rendered to the newly sovereign States. The civil service has often been called the 'iron frame' of India and Pakistan, and it has amply deserved the name. It has kept politicians on the rails, supported Ministers, converted vague dreams into practical programmes and, at times of crisis, it has been called upon to straighten out muddles and messes made in some of the state governments (as in East Punjab in India, or East Bengal in Pakistan) by irresponsible party politicians: the officials have had to take over and re-establish orderly government. Some members of the bureaucracy have been summoned to become Ministers themselves when no politician of suitable stature was forthcoming: Choudhri Mohammad Ali, an outstanding member of the old I.C.S., became Prime Minister of Pakistan at a particularly critical juncture; Sri Chintaman Deshmukh, another notable I.C.S. figure, became independent India's Finance Minister. In a new democracy politicians are not always noted for their representative qualities, and are certainly not easily held to account by the people. In these conditions a professional, responsible, independent civil service is as vital to the public interest as a representative legislature.

The relationship of the military to government is not often examined by writers on law, politics, or constitutional theory, but a professional, reliable, non-political army is another component of democracy. Whenever an army takes upon itself the task of government and politics, the end is almost inevitably dictatorship and the stifling of all opposition, as in KMT China, Peron's Argentina, or Nasser's Egypt. The idea of a non-political, professional army is not well-established in world practice. Wellington's army was both amateur and involved in politics; the French and German armies were highly professional but, right up to the Second World War, both attempted to play a part in politics. A tradition of keeping right out of political matters was deeply implanted in the British-Indian army; indeed, the officer class was too much withdrawn from political activity in the outside world. This may be partly ascribed to the army's responsibility for internal security in India; there was a deep suspicion that any officer who took upon himself a political decision would find himself attacked by Indian politicians and abandoned by British civil officials. The case of General Dyer at Amritsar was always remembered. This aloofness has been followed to a remarkable extent in both the armies of India and Pakistan since independence.[7] No democracy has yet shown itself able to dispense with a reserve of armed force with which to maintain order in an emergency. Unless the army accepts an

---

[7] The Rawalpindi conspiracy case, involving a high-ranking Pakistani army officer was the exception that proves the rule.

allegiance higher than that of governments and parties, a loyalty to the established law of the state, it will not be prepared to intervene—and then withdraw when normality is restored. The record of the Pakistan army in the Lahore riots of 1953, when ministerial rule collapsed in the face of religious fanaticism, shows that its higher loyalty is equal to the test. Without doubt, the Indian army is equally staunch.

The British-Indian system of higher education has often been criticised. It concentrated on literary subjects derived from English patterns of study, subjects which had no relation to Indian life. It encouraged students to memorise and recapitulate the contents of textbooks without any attempt being made to impel the students to apply their minds towards a true understanding of their subjects. All this is true of Indian universities in the mass : but it is not the whole truth. Hundreds of thousands of youths crammed or idled, dragged themselves through or failed their B.A. as a wearisome but inescapable preliminary to the procurement of any sort of decent job. But among their number, thousands of youths attended well-founded colleges and underwent courses in Law, Economics or History, which provided genuine standards and ideals and a pattern of thought.

In almost every emergent Asian nation the principal bottle-neck, the key to all other shortcomings and problems, is a shortage of trained manpower; a lack of men and women trained to think and decide; capable of absorbing new ideas and of operating new techniques. India has such a shortage, but it is nothing like so acute as in other newly independent countries. India is even capable of supplying certain categories of trained personnel, such as doctors, to other more needy Asian countries. All this means that India has just about enough leaders to make democracy work : the public servants, planners, politicians, leaders of opinion are just about adequate in numbers and in quality : and they are mainly the products of the Indian universities.

In the same way, while it is easy to discern much that is harmful in the Indian press, it also contains a leaven of quality which works for the fostering of democracy. At first inspection, the Indian press looks thoroughly rotten. There are hundreds of papers whose circulation is tiny, continuously on the verge of bankruptcy; kept going by recourse to the wildest sensationalism and personal attacks upon persons in public places, attacks which are often a thin cover for blackmail. Even the larger papers are frequently capable of apparently completely cynical irresponsibility, as well as debased emotionalism in their reaction to any internal or international event which is not to their taste. Yet the press has played a vital part in political development. In the days of official rule it maintained a constant pressure upon the autocratic administration, forcing it along in the direction of national emancipation. Some journals (such as the Allahabad *Leader*) were standard-bearers of social reform and regeneration. Today, amid a welter of abuse and spite, there are a dozen papers in India, notably the *Statesman,* the *Hindu,* and the *Times of India,* which maintain the function of guardians of sanity, equity and social justice against the sometimes hysterical, often tyrannical behaviour of party bosses.

A free democracy (as opposed to a 'People's Democracy') must be safeguarded by an independent judiciary to determine, as the English judges have determined for centuries, what is law and what the State may and may not require of the citizen. Electorates may be fooled or flattered, parliaments may, perhaps, be suborned; but an established bench of judges whose tenure is secure, and who know and cherish the law, and are ready to defend it, is a powerful guarantee of freedom and justice.

The Rule of Law as a principle has been accepted and exalted by Indian nationalists. It rests not so much upon detailed acceptance of the English common law as upon acceptance of the spirit of the common law. *Mandamus, Quo Warranto, Ultra Vires, Habeas Corpus*: these are now as much native to India as to Britain (the same being true of Pakistan, Ceylon, Burma or Ghana). The new India has gone further than the British ever did in underlining the independent authority of the judiciary. The British, after initial experimentation, kept on much of the pre-existing Indian structure of local legal administration, which was based upon the district official, an executive

officer who also dispensed justice. So the British Deputy Commissioner or Collector was both head of the district administration and also a magistrate : to some extent, a judge in his own
cause. But the independent Government of India has renounced
its own past in favour of the separation of the judiciary and
the executive. Today's District Officer is excluded completely
from participation in the judicial process. India has also taken
great care to safeguard the independence of the judges by insert-
ing detailed clauses into the Constitution.

And so India has assimilated and incorporated all the English
experience of centuries of free institutions into her own political
framework, evolving a democracy that is not only a great idea
but is also flesh and blood reality. But independence was not
approached through the assimilation of English institutions only :
indeed, the last years of British rule were marked by incessant
revolt and a flat rejection of the British programme for constitutional advance.

The early history of the Indian national movement shows a
definite policy of acquiring 'political education' by leaders such
as Dadabhai Naoroji and G. K. Gokhale. They stressed India's
need to obtain experience of the working of legislative councils,
municipalities and district boards before self-government could
become a possibility. Under the influence of Tilak, and even
more of Gandhi, these constitutional methods were jettisoned
and campaigns of mass agitation were substituted to force the
British government to surrender power as and when the nationalists demanded. During the years 1920 to 1937 the Dyarchy
experiment was launched, whereby the provincial legislatures
were expanded to form broadly representative bodies, with
Ministers responsible to the legislatures in charge of all the
'nation building' subjects (education, public health, local government, etc.). But only a small minority of the nationalist politicians, notably the Liberals, were prepared to tackle the task of
making the scheme work. The Indian National Congress, following Gandhi's lead, devoted its energies to trying to bring
government to the edge of anarchy. Even when leaders other
than Gandhi were in the ascendant, when the policy of boycott

was partially modified, the Congress was prepared to contest elections only so as to enter the legislatures for the purpose of sabotaging ministerial government, to 'wreck' Dyarchy. This policy was justified by appeals to Indian sentiments, but it is hard to resist the conclusion that the example of Ireland was the main cause of this lapse into negation. Ireland had been plunged into a chaos of guerrilla warfare, arson and assassination, until law and order had utterly collapsed : only then did the British Government accede to Ireland's demands (subject to the separation of Ulster) in 1921. The lesson that India read into these events was that Britain would relinquish power only in the face of violence. In consequence, the last quarter-century of British rule in India was marred by bitterness, hatred and frustration ; of mass campaigns which were non-violent in origin but which almost always degenerated into riot and destruction, leading to police retaliation, mass arrests, and incarceration for the leaders. It seems probable that this prolongation of struggle and deadlock did little or nothing to hasten on the process of emancipation, and may actually have delayed its achievement : in Ceylon the national leaders readily co-operated in making the reforms work, even when the constitutional changes fell short of their aspirations : and Ceylon achieved full independence at the same moment as India and Pakistan.[8]

Perhaps the only fruitful result of the Congress emphasis upon militancy and direct action was the emotional liberation which appears to have followed. The experience of colonial rule, it is frequently asserted, fastens a 'slave mentality' upon the colonial subject. He degenerates into a passive attitude to the world which inhibits him from tackling his problems; instead, he surrenders action and decision to the colonial master, whom he comes to regard with a malicious mixture of servility and assertiveness. Whether or not colonial rule does generate quite such a degrading attitude, there is clearly an unequal, unnatural

[8] This thesis is cogently developed in Jennings, *The Approach to Self-Government*, 1956, especially in Chapter 12, 'The Transition.' Sir Ivor Jennings suggests that Ceylon might actually have obtained independence earlier (in 1945) had not the turmoil in India discouraged the British Government from pressing on with constitutional reforms for India's next-door neighbour.

relationship between the rulers and the ruled. The various challenges to British rule staged between 1921 and 1942, involving as they did a defiance of British authority and an exaltation of the spirit of Indian freedom, must have contributed towards liberating Indian intellectuals from any physical or emotional sense of inferiority or impotence induced by more than a hundred years of foreign domination. During the course of the struggle an unhealthy quantity of hatred and suspicion was generated, but the very intensity of the struggle, followed by the clean, sharp severing of ties with the former suzerain in 1947, may have served to purge nationalist Indians of their bitterness towards the British. At any rate, most Indians of stature, following the noble example of Pandit Nehru, have been able to put away rancour and embark upon a useful relationship of equality and co-operation with the former imperial power. Independence was won on terms of mutual self-respect : it was not accorded by the overlord as a favour, but neither was it wrested from him by actual armed conflict. Political India was able to turn to the problem of adapting the British legacy of institutions of government, without having to make too many purely emotional gestures.

In the sterile quarter-century of non-co-operation there was one brief, constructive interlude. Under the 1935 Government of India Act Dyarchy was replaced by unfettered provincial ministerial government. Congress, having condemned the Act as completely reactionary, proceeded to contest the elections ' to combat the Act and seek the end of it.' Congress emerged from the 1936 elections with a clear majority in five provinces and near-majorities in three others : only in the Muslim-majority provinces did the non-Congress politicians achieve any success. After considerable debate, the Congress High Command decided to sanction the formation of Congress Cabinets and Governments in the eight provinces : these governments functioned until the end of 1939 when they resigned at the behest of the High Command in protest against the Viceroy's action in making India a party to the war against Germany without consulting the Indian nation. The thinking of the Congress cabinet ministers underwent a fundamental change during their two years of office. At first their aim was to put an end to the evils of British bureaucracy: they encouraged party members in the districts to prepare complaints against officials, and soon these were being investigated by innumerable Congress committees of inquiry. But these pursuits rapidly lost their fascination. Professor Laski once sagely observed that 'men who get their hands on an administrative machine become concerned to exploit its full possibilities merely by learning what they are.' The Congress ministries found that they really could make the machine do what they wanted: they began to evolve plans for social reconstruction, and then they discovered that attempts to carry out their plans through the use of the Congress party machine did not work: they needed the trained officials (whose time was being consumed in answering charges of tyranny) to make their plans a reality. And so the investigations lapsed, and within a few months Congress ministers and British bureaucrats were working together as a team in the Whitehall or Canberra fashion, completely ignoring the brickbats and *lathi* blows which they had directed at each other only a little while before. The Congress ministers discovered that the administrative machine really was a public service, and not a mere instrument of oppression. In parliament they found that laws and budgets had some virtue; they began to savour the quality of parliamentary activities as a real medium of political expression.

The period had its negative side: in particular, the contemptuous depreciation by the Congress of the Muslim League, together with equivocal behaviour towards Muslim institutions and individuals, which did much to stimulate the movement for Pakistan. Nevertheless, this period gave the future leaders of the nation a unique opportunity to gain experience of parliament and government (many ministers were distinctly reluctant to abandon the experience when ordered to resign by the High Command). This phase was invaluable in giving the leaders of the future a firm foundation from which to create the institutions of government for the new India.[9]

9 Morris-Jones, *op. cit.*, pp. 66ff.

10

At the time of the transfer of power, the British Government made no attempt to prefabricate constitutions for India and Pakistan : the only provision made was the designation of the 1935 Act as an interim instrument of government. The new Indian Constitution did not come into operation until January 26, 1950. A recent study of Tilak and Indian political philosophy concludes, wryly, that 'there is no reflection of Indian precepts or political philosophy in the Indian Constitution' : it is built up entirely from concepts taken from Anglo-Saxon political history.[10] It is not, perhaps, so surprising that Indian leaders adopted the political, constitutional and legal principles which were so familiar to them as members of the Inns of Court or graduates of British or British-Indian universities. The Philippines, Indonesia, the States of Indo-China : as each attained its freedom, forms of government peculiar to each particular metropolitan power were adopted by the new States. But in some cases, these loans were of a very temporary nature. Within a brief period Indonesia had abrogated the Netherlands-Indonesian Union, while the States of Indo-China promptly quitted the French Union : yet India, Pakistan and Ceylon remain full members of the Commonwealth, despite the Suez War. Then, Vietnam, which began with a ceremonial Head of State on the French model, now has an Executive Head of State ; Indonesia, which adopted parliamentary, cabinet government, as in the Netherlands, has never made a success of the system and, at the time of writing, experiments are being made in 'guided democracy' with President Sukarno as leader and guide. But in the former British dominions, despite the desperate difficulties encountered in Pakistan, parliamentary, cabinet government continues and develops.

The Constitution of the Indian Union is probably the longest document of its kind in the world : 250 pages, or 395 articles. By an odd paradox the detested 1935 Act provided its main basis, supplying many paragraphs almost verbatim : and the 1935 Act was the most voluminous measure ever passed by the British

---

[10] T. L. Shay, *The Legacy of the Lokamanya: The Political Philosophy of Bal Gangadhar Tilak,* 1956, p. 167.

parliament. This labyrinthine constitution includes parts devoted to citizenship, fundamental rights, and directive principles of State policy, as well as the parts providing for the processes of government.[11] Whereas British rule in India focussed upon the Governor-General as executive head of government, the high authority of independent India is the sovereign parliament. Vast residual powers are vested in the president, but the convention firmly established by President Prasad is one of almost complete aloofness from actual administration. Although India has a federal constitution, 'States' Rights' are not venerated as in the United States. State governments may be (and have been) suspended by Presidential proclamation; state boundaries may be (and have been) altered or obliterated by notification of the central government. This apparent contradiction of a federal government which is strongly centralised is easily explicable in the light of history. The British unified India and brought it under a strong central government: the Congress party developed a highly centralised caucus, the so-called High Command. There were forces making for decentralisation, especially the variety of communities throughout the sub-continent, but the first years of independence have seen power concentrated at the centre, with Nehru and his cabinet. The process of unification has been carried much further by the liquidation of the former Princely states, whose territories covered almost half the face of undivided India (British India, 886,000 square miles; Indian states, 690,000 square miles). These 562 states—some mere villages, some sizable countries, but all relics of a feudal, medieval India—have been merged into greater units or (as in the case of Hyderabad) divided upon linguistic lines. Their very names have vanished from the map, with only one exception, Mysore.

If this somewhat ruthless rationalisation of the map of India appears to provide evidence of an authoritarian trend in Congress India, as some foreign observers assert, the record of the functioning of parliament and parliamentary elections offers convincing proof of the reality of democracy in India.

---

[11] Of Part IV, Principles of State Policy, Sir Ivor Jennings observes that 'The ghosts of Sidney and Beatrice Webb stalk through the text.' It is Socialism without Socialisation. Jennings, *Some Characteristics of the Indian Constitution*, 1953, p. 31.

The Indian political scene takes its colour largely from the continued predominance of Congress over all other parties. Many expected that with the attainment of independence Congress would dissolve into different and differing groups according to the interests which, it was alleged, made up the movement. A tripartite division was often prophesied. The followers of Gandhi were expected to challenge the westernisation of India by a programme of truly Indian social reform, typified in the cult of the *charka*, the Indian spinning wheel. In the field of politics they would call for a revival of the *panchayat* (see p. 87, *ante*), and in the field of economics they would emphasise the fostering of village industries. Pandit Nehru was expected to lead a Socialist Party with a Marxist programme of planning and State industries. The forces of the Right were usually linked with the name of Sardar Patel, and it was assumed that conservative, orthodox Hindus would somehow combine with big business to oppose the policies identified with Gandhi and Nehru.

In actuality, this splitting of Congress did not occur, except on a minor scale. Whether Gandhi would have wished to enter the political lists with his *charka* philosophy may be doubted : as it was, his assassination was followed by the involvement of his followers in the *Bhoodan* movement in which Gandhi's disciple, Vinoba Bhave, launched his 'land gift' campaign, a complete departure from politics. The Right-wingers lost their most considerable representative with the death of Sardar Patel : Dr. S. P. Mukherji resigned from the Cabinet and seceded from Congress in 1951 to form the Rightist *Jan Sangh*, but he too died in 1953. Pandit Nehru, the protagonist of Socialism, has maintained his leadership at a national and not a party level. Jaiprakash Narayan, perhaps in order of importance the second Congress Socialist leader, abandoned politics to participate in *Bhoodan*. Another leading Socialist, Acharya Kripalani, did resign from Congress to form a dissident radical party, *Kisan Mazdoor Praja*, which was amalgamated with the Socialist Party. This gain in strength was balanced by the secession of dissident Socialists led by Dr. Lohia. Congress under Nehru has continued to command general allegiance as the accepted government of India.

In all probability this is because there is a general consensus of opinion on policy: Conservatives and Socialists, industrialists and clerks, all alike agree that India must be developed to attain a more productive, more diversified economy. In the conditions which prevail today, all agree that planning, together with forms of State control are essential: private enterprise cannot possibly create the new industries, the irrigation projects, the improved communications which are needed. There is also general agreement on foreign policy: on 'peaceful co-existence,' on the importance of the UN, and—unfortunately—on the need to oppose Pakistan over Kashmir. And so the government is able to command a very wide circle of co-operation and agreement in its present policy.

The first requirement for an understanding of present-day politics is an appreciation of this spirit of agreement: the continued predominance of Congress as the expression of this spirit then becomes acceptable as a thoroughly democratic feature. If the actual working of parliament, and the procedure at elections are scrutinised, these are seen to contain much of the essential spirit of democracy. Congress commands an unassailable majority in the parliament at Delhi. It is assumed in Britain that an overwhelming majority in parliament does not

House of the People: Distribution of Seats

	After first General Election.	After Second Election.
Congress	364	366
Communists	16	29
Socialists/K.M.P.	21	18§
Jan Sangh	3	4
Other parties and independents	85	71§

§ 6 dissident Socialists included with 'others.'

make either for good government or for a healthy political climate; two parties, alternately filling the roles of government and opposition are regarded as both desirable and normal. But such conditions are not necessarily equally desirable in Asia, where in a newly independent country the greatest asset is a

national party with a stable majority in parliament. Burma,
despite internal civil war and foreign invasion, has remained a
viable State largely because of the solidarity of the governing
Anti-Fascist People's Freedom League.   On the other hand,
Pakistan has had to face crisis after crisis, following the wilting
away of the Muslim League, because no party has commanded
a decisive following.   Indonesia, with a multiplicity of parties
and factions has endured a series of phantom governments until
finally power has passed from the politicians to the army.   In
the previous chapter it was argued (p. 88) that Asian thought
is grounded in the belief that the community should make its
decisions by finding a general area of agreement rather than by
adopting a majority vote—which may leave a sizable dissenting
minority.   Thus, the long muster-roll of Congress has strengthened rather than weakened the initial growth of parliamentary
democracy in India.

The Congress leaders, moreover, are passionately concerned
to make parliament a reality.   It is significant that the Government Chief Whip holds the appointment of Minister for Parliamentary Affairs, and great care is given to transacting parliamentary business according to form and precedent.   Professor
Morris-Jones, having observed the members in session, remarks
that ' to an increasing extent they are learning that they must
listen to others if their own contributions are to be effective, that
they must debate, not merely address.'   The actual promotion
of legislation, he notes, is largely initiated and worked out by the
civil service, nevertheless, ' the contribution of Parliament has
not been negligible—in getting the big issues stated, the details
scrutinised and the interests of affected parties heard.' [12]

Perhaps because their majority is so assured, and although
voting discipline is strict, Congress members frequently criticise
and question the actions of their government and its agents.[13]
There is nothing like the slavish adherence to official party policy
which prevails in the British House of Commons.   Question
time is a vigorous institution : more vigorous than in some older

[12] Morris-Jones, *op. cit.*, p. 323.
[13] *op. cit.*, p. 196.

parliaments, like those of Australia and New Zealand. A special feature is the Half an Hour Discussion, whereby twice a week time is set aside so that members can raise some important topic (subject to the Speaker's consent) which it is felt has not been adequately dealt with at question time. In addition, Friday is set aside for private members' business, as in the House of Commons.

Whether the Indian system eventually develops its own special checks and balances and means of calling governments to task, or whether a two-party system after the British form will one day be established is as yet unknown. There is little doubt as to the Indian view of the matter: the parliamentarians are almost unanimous in wishing for the development of a strong opposition as a necessary component of parliamentary responsibility.[14] It seems not improbable that when the unique personality of Nehru is at length withdrawn from the political arena the opposition parties will find their task of eroding the Congress majority much simplified. The verdict of the first two General Elections, however, provides little indication as to where this opposition is going to be found.

The decision to hold a General Election at the end of 1951 on the basis of adult franchise—which produced an electorate of 190 millions—was characterised by President Prasad as 'an act of faith.' This was interpreted by foreign reporters as implying a leap in the dark, but the President meant that India could have faith in the people to exercise their vote in a responsible manner. In another sense the decision was an act of faith—in the civil service—for upon the officials fell the incalculable task of making the elections possible. Just as one example of a hundred difficulties in the preliminary stages: the preparation of electoral rolls was impeded by the fact that most Indian women find it unthinkable to pronounce their husband's name to any outsider. There was the problem of devising a fool-proof and knave-proof voting procedure; the problem of staffing thousands of polling-stations in order that voters should not have to trudge

14 *op. cit.*, p. 270, n.l.

too many miles; the problem of ensuring secrecy to the ballot; the problem of conveying the ballot-boxes to headquarters speedily and with adequate precautions against irregularities en route; the problem of counting the hundreds of thousands of votes and of recording the results; and above all, the problem of convincing the public and the politicians that this whole complicated process was honest and impartial. In the end the job was done: the price was the complete dislocation of the administration for many months on end.

One hundred and six million persons cast their votes, equal to 55 per cent of the electorate. Despite the Congress landslide, the popular vote was by no means so favourable: they received 45 per cent of the total as compared to 11 per cent for the Socialists and 3 per cent for the Communists, who won dividends in actual seats by concentrating their campaign. Certain other features were significant: there was the resounding failure of all parties playing upon religious and communal prejudice, there was the failure of Dr. Ambedkar's Depressed Classes Federation to win seats reserved for the untouchables, there was the almost complete eclipse of the Muslims, apart from the return of a few hand-picked Congress Muslims. Independents gained a number of seats, usually winning on local reputation or prestige: sometimes, allegedly, because of economic pressure exerted on the electors. Many independents climbed aboard the Congress bandwagon after being returned. In general, the electorate showed considerable political acumen and *sens du possible* in rejecting the extremists and the woolly-minded.

The second elections, held in the early months of 1957, showed few important changes. The electors slightly increased their vote of confidence in Congress: from 47 to 54 million votes, a rise of from 45 to 46.5 per cent of the total. The Communists trebled their support (11 millions, previously 3½ millions), their share of the poll increasing from 3 to 10 per cent. The Socialist vote fell by one-third. There was an overall increase in the popular vote by about 11 millions: 60 per cent of the electorate went to the polls in 1957.

The foreign press concentrated upon the Communist success,

but a Communist share of the total vote which amounts to 10 per cent remains modest, say, by comparison with Communist strength in Western Europe. Surely the principal lesson of the elections is the unshaken supremacy of Congress? It is also noteworthy that even at the second election, despite weaknesses caused by disruptions in the party, the Socialists managed to maintain a small lead in terms of popular support over the more dynamic Communists. Apart from their fissile weaknesses, the Socialists suffer from the disadvantage that Congress can always say 'Anything you can promise—we can do better.' The Socialist Party still appears to carry the Congress label without the advantages of office : yet their day may come, when Nehru's titanic name at last disappears from the Congress posters.

Meanwhile, Communism provides the only important alternative mystique. In terms of practical politics, Communist policy concentrates on winning power in limited areas : after the 1957 state elections the Communists managed to secure a bare majority in one state, Kerala (formerly Travancore-Cochin). It is said of this area that even the dustmen are matriculates, and all the bus-conductors are graduates : this exposes the larger danger to democratic freedom, the strange compulsion which Communism exercises over the minds of so many Asian intellectuals. The under-privileged are, of course, susceptible, but the middle and upper classes are also drawn by the mystique, and for them the fascination is focussed in Communist China. Why is the land of brain-washing, mass-murder and social regimentation regarded with such admiration by westernised, constitutionally-minded upper and middle class Indians and other Asians? Clearly it is important to attempt to discover the source of this attraction in order to try to assess its potential influence in the future of democracy in Asia.

First, let us survey the Chinese Communist Revolution from the somewhat unsympathetic Western European viewpoint. Communist policy during the early years appears to have been phased as follows : 1949–51, a time when the Party bid for national support ; 1951–53, the Terror, when reactionary elements were liquidated ; 1953–56, the consolidation of the regime ;

and from 1957, perhaps, a period of 'de-Stalinisation' or relaxation of emphasis upon the State. During the first phase the propaganda line seemed designed to convince the Chinese that the main object of the Communists was to liberate the country from the legacy of the KMT, introducing efficiency and light into government. This was the time of the physical cleaning-up of cities, reform of the civil service, the overhauling of the railways. These reforms gained the Communists a large measure of adherence, especially from the professional classes, civil servants, doctors and university teachers, together with a certain acceptance by landlords and capitalists, as well as the goodwill of 'uncommitted' foreign governments. After the outbreak of the Korean War, the American drive to the Yalu, and the large-scale intervention of Chinese 'volunteers,' a complete change came over the scene. Influenced partly, perhaps, by fear of American invasion and by the activities of KMT saboteurs within China, the government launched the Terror. The so-called 'Five Antis,' *Wu Fan,* formed the basis for a campaign of denunciation and liquidation.[15] The groups specially selected for elimination included corrupt officials, landlords, rich peasants, shopkeepers, middle-men, and some Christians, more especially foreign missionaries. Not all the members of these groups suffered equally : some were permitted to save their skins by public confession and self-denunciation, surrender of goods and property, and submission to a process of re-education. Most had to undergo accusation at workers' meetings, trial before the People's Courts, mass demands for the extreme penalty, and public execution. Those killed were numbered in millions : the Communists themselves have put on record a figure of two million, British estimates, compiled in Hongkong, speak of three million dead, American figures run to eight million, and KMT estimates claim that fifteen million were murdered. Probably three million at least must have perished as a grim lesson to the Chinese people that no departure from Communist doctrine would be tolerated. Probably fifteen million others are toiling

---

[15] Anti-bribery, anti-evasion of taxes, anti-fraud, anti-theft of state property, anti-communication of state economic secrets.

as slave-labourers under suspended death sentence or under life sentence, on public works projects, in the mines, or in the factories.

Then came total mobilisation of the propaganda machine, and accelerated collectivisation of the land and nationalisation of industry. This programme appears to have been completed ahead of schedule, and has resulted in spectacular claims for increased production. Perhaps in consequence, reports from China in mid-1957 speak of a relaxation of controls and a measure of freedom for the individual. There is talk of a campaign to eliminate bureaucracy, of the admission of a certain amount of discussion in books and journals, of the lifting of the standing orders to all writers, journalists and teachers to write and lecture only upon 'democratic' themes—such as the achievements of the new industries, or the solidarity of the army with the peasants—in favour of more personal, subjective themes.

But where, it may be asked, does democracy enter into the picture? Here the argument becomes involved in semantics, because the word 'democracy' is attached to almost every institution in China today. The whole Communist system is called 'Democratic Centralism' or 'the People's Democratic Dictatorship.' The first cycle of Communist rule is called 'The New Democracy.' The officially recognised opposition styles itself 'The Democratic League.' Democracy, it seems, is everywhere, and the effect of its constant evocation upon the inexpert foreigner should not be summarily dismissed.[16] Unless these institutions are viewed with the eyes of faith, their democratic content appears chimerical. China is ruled by a Central People's Government Council, a closed party presidium, whose Chairman is Mao Tse-tung. There is the usual Marxist bureaucratic hierarchy—councils, committees, ministries—all, virtually, party apparatus. The Judiciary is headed by a Supreme Court and Procurator General's Office. The former KMT laws and decrees

---

[16] Compare the fact that the Indian National Congress, being so named, was regarded by most Americans and some Europeans—during the British period—as identical with the United States Congress : a sovereign assembly. The effect upon the American attitude to the Indian Congress's claims was considerable.

were immediately abolished, and judgments are now awarded on an *ad hoc* basis whereby law and punishment are determined by the Communist judges according to the requirements of the day. Alice queried whether you can make words mean different things, to which Humpty Dumpty replied, 'The question is, which is to be master—that's all.' In Communist China there is no question : the State is always master.

There is one form of national assembly called the Chinese People's Political Consultative Conference. It was first set up in 1949, and given its present shape at the end of 1953 when the members were elected by various prescribed local organisations : it contains 1,200 members of whom 668 are Communists, 274 belong to the Democratic League (which has a vague working relationship with the Communist Party) and 258 who are non-party. 150 seats have been allotted to minorities and thirty to overseas Chinese. The Conference functions on a basis of co-existence and co-operation between the parties, who have unanimously adopted the 'Common Programme' which lays down general policy : in a Communist State, all correct political thought is necessarily in accord with Marxist doctrine : on these terms, the Conference serves a purpose in providing a sounding-board for announcements of policy.

Political activity at lower levels is virtually party propaganda. The most important agency is the system of cadres, *kan pu* ; young, enthusiastic, highly-trained party members who carry propaganda into the fields, the factories and the armed forces ; their training with its intensive indoctrination, discussion and self-criticism has been often described.[17] The collectivisation programme includes provision for co-operative committees formed among the cultivators. Villages and towns are divided into neighbourhood units, 'lane associations,' charged with the task of keeping their little areas clean, and with checking anti-social practices among the householders. Perhaps these activities allow a modicum of genuine discussion and association ; but it is difficult to detect much else that can be stretched so as to be

---

[17] Perhaps the best account is that of R. Walker, *China Under Communism, the First Five Years.*

labelled 'democratic,' as the word is understood in London, Washington or Canberra—or in Delhi, Karachi, Colombo or Manilla.

It is no part of this writer's purpose to pursue the argument that the present Communist regime represents a vast conspiracy to enslave China : so far as can be judged, the regime has the solid support of the Chinese people. In Mao Tse-tung it has a leader who is one of the world's giants. Possessing a deep knowledge of Confucian teaching, the penetrating vision of a poet, and a firm, practical mastery of Marxist dialectic, he is evolving a new order which is firmly rooted in the history and tradition of the Middle Kingdom, yet is achieving rapid strides towards economic and social development on a scale never dreamed of before. All this is undoubted : but it does not alter the fact that present-day China offers the biggest challenge to free institutions that has yet arisen in the world.

How then to explain the spell which China exercises over liberal-minded intellectuals in the 'uncommitted' countries of Asia? Let us return to the word Equality. China has enhanced the value of this word throughout Asia. As a nation, China has achieved full equality with the most advanced States of the world; as a land of many communities, China offers equality to the non-Chinese social groups; and in the ranks of the new social order China offers equality of opportunity to her sons and daughters.

As a nation, the China of yesterday seemed to be the most dismal example of the backwardness of Asia : in international politics, a cypher; in economic terms, a pre-industrial society with few railways or power resources and an import-export mechanism entirely foreign-controlled. Within eight years all this has been changed. In international relations China has negotiated on terms of complete equality with the Western Powers at Geneva. Russia is no more the mentor, but rather, in the months after the Hungarian revolt, humbly grateful that China was prepared to use her influence to repair breaches in the Soviet satellite system. The results of the first phase of economic development have been spectacular : steel production has been quadrupled in four years, motor vehicles designed and built in China are rolling off the assembly line, mighty dams and power projects promise a vast increase in arable land and electric energy. All this is impressive, even to Indians with their own Five Year Plan; to South East Asia it comes as a revelation of what a backward Asian country can achieve by utilising Asian men and materials. Finally, there were the Chinese battles with the American and other UN forces in North Korea. This is not a topic which all Asians, by any means, delight to dwell upon: but these battles (which in many Asian eyes were Chinese victories over the Westerners) have their place in the search for equality. Asian psychological reflexes, reacting against the 'slave mentality,' seem at times to create crude anti-Western spitefulness, as deleterious in its way as the arrogance and egocentricity of the West, now at last on the wane. The emotional reaction against the West is fed by Chinese military and diplomatic successes. China has tackled the West on its own terms and has shown that Asians are equal to Americans or Europeans upon the field of battle or at the conference table. China has been quick to exploit the Asian yearning for equality and status in the world today by well-staged gestures. The Prime Minister, Chou En-lai, is assiduous in his visits to other Asian countries where his silver tongue finds the apt phrase of felicitation upon emancipation from colonial bondage and offers promises of China's support and sympathy in future development. Asian guests from prime ministers down to students are constantly invited to China, conducted on tours of inspection of the new works of welfare and development, and encouraged to feel that all this is part of their destiny.

Chinese policy towards the non-Chinese communities within their ambit has also undergone a revolution. Traditionally, the Chinese regarded their non-Chinese vassals as 'barbarians' who could only be accepted as equals if they civilised themselves by accepting the Chinese language, ethics, institutions and government. This policy gave China a reputation for imperialism in the borderlands of South and South East Asia, and there was prolonged resistance by the border peoples to the process of

Sinoization.[18] Now all is changed: the People's Republic has implemented a policy of local autonomy for the minorities—who are said to amount to a total of sixty millions. The leading minority, the Mongols, in addition to having their own inter-nationally-recognised State, the Mongolian People's Republic (formerly claimed, though never effectively administered by Nationalist China) also enjoy a separate government within China, the Inner Mongolian Autonomous Region. In 1957, another Muslim people, the Chuangs or Tungans, were also reported to be forming a similar Chuang Autonomous Region. Other races, such as the Tai, have smaller 'autonomous' units down to the district level. Whatever may be the measure of local self-government permitted, there is no doubt that cultural autonomy is fully encouraged. Local languages, literature, music and other arts are afforded considerable State support, while university faculties have, for the first time, created departments for the study of the cultures of the minorities. The Communist occupation of Tibet and recent penetration (1953–57) on the north-east frontier of Burma have been headlined in the Western press as evidence of a Chinese policy of expansion. The govern-ments of India and Burma (perhaps with inner reservations) have expressed themselves as unperturbed by these activities: the policy of local autonomy for the frontier peoples may have helped to reassure China's neighbours as to whether this penetration was imperialist or democratic. Certainly, at the Bandung Con-ference, Chou En-lai attempted to exploit the Communist policy of equality for the non-Chinese peoples as evidence of China's peaceful intentions in South East Asia.

Finally, there is the egalitarianism of the new China. Chinese society up to the downfall of the KMT was stratified both hori-zontally and vertically. There was the gentry class, the scholars and officials, whose position in society was superior and privi-leged. Merchants, being uneducated persons, were low down upon the social ladder, and the peasants were lowest of all;

---

[18] For a more detailed study of these border peoples, in the past and at present, see the present writer's paper in *Pacific Affairs*, xxix, December 1956, 'Burma's North-east Borderland Problems.'

human animals, fit for toil and nothing more. The 'vertical' divisions were a result of the provincial, local quality of Chinese society which produced an infinite number of guilds and secret societies, exclusive organisations which excluded, actively, all would-be intruders. The effect of the Chinese Communist Revolution was to transform China into a society mainly concerned with the welfare of the peasant and the labourer. There is a tremendous concentration upon making the village a better place and the villagers real members of the community. It is also a society where advancement is open to all : indeed, priority of opportunity for higher and technical education is deliberately given to youngsters from the families of peasants and workers. The much-publicised austerity of the managerial classes, typified in the universal adoption of the 'boiler suit' may be assumed or real : but it is sufficiently genuine to form a shining contrast to the luxuries of the KMT millionaire-politicians—or indeed to the ostentatious style of living enjoyed by the governing classes in certain 'free' Asian countries, such as Siam or the Philippines.

In an Asia where 'democracy' is almost automatically equated with the battle against Western imperialism, the struggle for economic betterment, and the cult of 'the people,' the peasant and the worker, China stands high indeed as a symbol of democracy.

But (as this essay has tried to show) another and truer form of democracy has been established in India. That is the pattern which a number of other Asian States seek to follow. Asia today is a massive political reality. Outsiders who view the greatest of the six continents merely as an appendage to the world domination of America and Russia are still viewing the world through late nineteenth century spectacles. Asia matters, for itself alone. The fate of its two largest nations, India and China, will largely influence the fate of Asia, and perhaps the fate of the world.

INDEX

Absolute monarch, 70
  Asia, 87
Absolute state, 5
Absolutism in Hellenistic monarchies, 46
Adenauer, Dr. Konrad, 13
  coalition government, 13
Afghanistan, 45
  absorption of democracy, 89
Africa, 65 *et seq.*
  Asian resistance to the West, 67
  chieftainship in, 74
  Christianity in, 67
  colonialism in, 90
  democratic institutions, 65 *et seq.*
    dangers to, 68
    development of, 74
    foreseeability of, 72
    tribe system, and, 71
  District Commissioner, 73
  ecclesiastical institutions, 82
  impact of Western ideas, 67
  introduction of central machinery of government, 76
  languages, 69
  paganism in, 67
  political systems, *see* Political system
  privilege of democracy in, 82
  relation to Europe in the past, 65
  suggested federal system, 77
African Political Systems, ed. Prof. M. Fortes and Prof. E. E. Evans-Pritchard, 69
Algeria, 7
Anti-clericalism, 12
Aristocratic principle of government, 80
Army in India and Pakistan, 129
Asia, 85 *et seq.*
  absolute monarch in, 87
  acceptance of British ideas, 97
  African reaction to the West, 67
  American prestige, 99
  cabinet system, 99
  Communism, appeal of, 93, 102
  democracy and poverty in, 103
  distribution of population, 94
  education in, 92
  government in, 86
  legislative councils in, 99
  lower class in, 93
  nationalism in, 111

Asia—*contd.*
  peasants
    income, 94
    vote, 96
  political development in, 91, 99
  resistance to Western influence, 66
  Russian example, 103
  struggle against colonialism, 90
  universal franchise in, 110
  upper middle class in, 92
  village self-government, 88
  Western conquests in, 89
Aung San, 104

Bagehot, Walter
  preface to *English Constitution,* 4
Balfour, Arthur, 4
Bantu
  language, 69
  tribes, 71
Belgian Congo, 79
Belgium,
  constitution of, 51
Bombay, 92
Britain
  attraction of political institutions of, 108
  General Strike in, 4
  large political parties in, 14
  national unity in, 6
  new middle classes, 9
  Rule of Law, 97
  working class, 10
British Central Africa,
  aristocratic policy in, 79
Buddhism,
  influence of
    Cambodia, 113
    Laos, 113
    Siam, 113
  law of, 97
  revival of, 113
Buganda,
  Kubaka, 70, 77
  political system of, 70
Bundestag, 13
Burma,
  civil war in, 111
  government in, 86
  social scale, 87
  solidarity of governing party, 140

Calcutta, 92

11